1991

NATURE AND GRACE
IN FLANNERY O'CONNOR'S FICTION

NATURE AND GRACE
IN FLANNERY O'CONNOR'S FICTION

Lorine M. Getz

Studies in Art and Religious Interpretation
Volume Two

The Edwin Mellen Press
New York and Toronto

Library of Congress Cataloging in Publication Data

Getz, Lorine M.
   Nature and grace in Flannery O'Connor's fiction.

   (Studies in art and religious interpretation ;
v. 2)
   Bibliography: p.
   Includes index.
   1. O'Connor, Flannery--Religion and ethics.
2. Grace (Theology) in literature. I. Title.
II. Series.
PS3565.C57Z678 1983   813'.54   82-22458
ISBN 0-88946-550-9

Studies in Art and Religious Interpretation
   ISBN 0-88946-956-3

            The Edwin Mellen Press
            P.O. Box 450
            Lewiston, New York   14092

Lorine Getz is executive director of the Boston Theological
Institute, co-chair of the Women's Caucus: Religious Studies,
and has published another book with the Edwin Mellen Press
entitled *Flannery O'Connor: Her Life, Library and Book Reviews.*

Printed in the United States of America

To my Sisters and Brothers

ACKNOWLEDGMENTS

This study, which began as part of a personal search and research project, became a "compulsion," perhaps even a "grace." During the decade required to bring it to completion, I have been helped and encouraged by many colleagues and friends who cannot all be mentioned here.

I am especially grateful to David Rosenfield who first introduced me to Flannery O'Connor's fiction; to my teachers and critics Frederick Asals, the late Arthur Gibson, John Meagher, and Herbert Richardson who read earlier versions of this manuscript and made valuable suggestions for improving it; to Delia Burke, Judith Eckelmeyer, Mareyjoyce Green and Diane Karpinski who listened supportively and creatively critiqued the developing project; to the Sisters of St. Joseph, especially Isabel and Marge, who fostered my theological studies; and to my parents Howard and Dorothy, and my brothers and sisters Howie, Sue, Kathy, Ken and Beth who in ways physical, intellectual, and spiritual sustained me through these long years of research.

Finally I wish to thank Beth Huber who typed the manuscript; David Kelly and Diane Culbertson who provided invaluable editorial assistance; my father, who proofread it; and Susan Reinbold who saw it through its final preparations for publication.

For whatever errors persist in the text, I am solely responsible.

Lorine M. Getz

Newton Center, MA
August, 1982

CONTENTS

INTRODUCTION

As religion and literature gradually began to separate themselves from their roots in myth, a void grew up between these two modes of human expression. Prior to the Enlightenment these two branches of knowledge were not studied separately: a theocentric approach embraced both the sacred and the profane sciences. The Enlightenment, however, led to a dissociation, even an opposition, between these two modes of exposition. Recognizing the inadequacy of such a separation, contemporary scholars from both disciplines have begun to establish a dialogue. The past generation has seen the emergence of "theologians of literature" and "literary theologians." Nathan Scott, Amos Wilder, Walter Ong, Sallie McFague (TeSelle), Tom Driver and others, representing the former group, have sought to analyze the implicit theological content of works of art and to understand the theological dimensions of the various literary forms themselves.[1] Among the self-conscious "literary theologians," persons who have sought to give artistic expression to theological themes, are T. S. Eliot, Fyodor Dostoevsky, François Mauriac, Graham Greene, Herman Hesse, and the subject of this study: Flannery O'Connor.

The emergence of self-conscious literary theologians is the counterface in the world of art to the emergence of scholars who are developing a theology of literature. Both groups have sought to expand the previous understandings of their genre. The literary didacticism of Eliot, Hesse and even O'Connor has at times been scorned in certain literary circles just as the theological eclecticism of Scott, Driver and others has led to their

---

[1] For an overview of contemporary religious-literary criticism, see Ruland, *Horizons of Criticism: An Assessment of Religious-Literary Options.*

1

depreciation in certain theological schools. But the emergence
of these new forms of literature and theology is important for
both disciplines, and the phenomenon deserves to be fully studied
and better understood.

Flannery O'Connor, who died in 1964, is acknowledged today
as one of the greatest American post-war writers of short stories.[2] Her writing is religious in nature and intent. In her

---

[2]Although not unanimous in their praise for O'Connor's work,
and unable to reach a consensus concerning the nature and meaning of her fiction, critics recognized O'Connor as a talented and
important young American short story writer from the beginning of
her publishing career. She received an extraordinary amount of
attention throughout her career, and the resulting body of secondary material leaves little doubt that her stories will continue to rank among the significant fiction of her era. See, for
example, Asals, "Flannery O'Connor as Novelist," pp. 23-39; Rubin,
"Flannery O'Connor and the Bible Belt," p. 51; and Stephens, *The
Question of Flannery O'Connor*, pp. 43-45. It has also been generally recognized that the second work, *The Violent Bear It Away*,
is more successful than the earlier, *Wise Blood*.
    For a surview of the critical material to 1976, see Golden,
"Flannery O'Connor." The early criticism, generally not of particular significance to our study, is found on pp. 13-38. As
Golden notes in his "Introduction," p. 5, some of this early
criticism was hostile. Golden, however, makes no distinction
between periods of critical opinion and suggests no reason for
this negative response. The early unfavorable reviews are generally concerned with the technical flaws in the first novel,
Wise Blood. One critic calls the novel a "brave, but unsuccessful attempt" (Davis, "Outraged, or Embarrassed," 1953); another
decries its lack of form and claims that the work has no thesis
(Creekmore, "A Southern Baptism," 1960). Other significant unfavorable articles and reviews represent confused attempts to
treat of the violence, provincialism, grotesquerie and religios-
ity of which O'Connor was accused. See, for example, La Farge,
"Manic Gloom," 1952; "Review of *A Good Man Is Hard to Find*," *New
Yorker*, 1955; Nyren, "Review of *The Violent Bear It Away*," 1960;
Esty, "In America, Intellectual Bomb Shelters," 1958; and Warnke,
"A Vision Deep and Narrow," 1960. Despite some serious negative
criticism, much of the secondary material which appeared in the
late 1950's and early 1960's praises O'Connor's technical skill:
her perfection of style, her keen eye for detail, her power in
delivery and her keen wit. See, for example, "Frustrated Preacher: A Review of *Wise Blood*," 1952; Steggert, "Review of *A Good
Man Is Hard to Find*," 1955; Charles, "Review of *The Violent Bear
It Away*," 1960; Engle and Hansford, eds., "Introduction," *Prize
Stories of 1955*, pp. 9-12; and "The Art of the Short Story,"
1957, pp. 176-191.

fiction she seeks to explicate her characters and plots in terms
of theological meaning. Her primary concern is the operation of
grace in the world, that moment of gratuitous interaction between
the divine and the human. She asserts that the action of grace
marks the definitive event in each person's life. She holds that
co-operation with God's grace is normative for the artist[3] and
that the reality of grace is especially suited for portrayal
through the narrative form.[4] Knowing that fiction is not capable
of portraying the essence of grace, but that it is able successfully to depict the operations of grace, she explores a wide
range of theological assertions concerning these encounters between God and human persons in her fiction.

Christian tradition has long investigated and agonized over
the relationship between human nature and God's grace in the plan
of redemption. It is not unusual, therefore, that an explicitly
Christian writer like Flannery O'Connor, whose fiction is directly concerned with the operations of grace among humankind, would
confront the central paradox. In what ways can God's grace be
understood to work within nature, building up the "natural order"
and thus contributing to the salvation of creation by a means
which harmoniously uplifts it? Conversely, to what extent must
grace be said to work against nature, opposing or rejecting it in
order to effect the salvation of a human nature deformed by sin?
For centuries theologians have tried to respond to this central
question. Some have emphasized the creative, humanizing or evolutionary, inherent aspects of grace: grace presupposes, builds on
and ennobles nature. Others have tended rather to underline the
effects of human sin, which reduces nature to its fallen state,
resistant to the grace of Christ: the Spirit wars against the
Flesh. No simple solution is possible.

Our study will be an investigation of the theology of grace

---

[3]*Mystery and Manners: The Occasional Prose of Flannery
O'Connor*, p. 27.

[4]*Mystery and Manners*, p. 118.

depicted in the fictional writings of Flannery O'Connor. The
focal questions will be: (1) What literary devices does O'Connor
use to depict the workings of grace in her fiction? (2) What concept or concepts of grace does O'Connor portray? (3) Can O'Connor
be said to have a single theology of grace in her fictional writings, or does she, in fact, have several theologies of grace?

Flannery O'Connor seeks to treat an aspect of human existence which is intrinsically difficult to depict and to render
intelligible. Her own presentation of the workings of grace is
complex and varies depending on her utilization of various literary devices. For these reasons, we will not seek to *abstract* one
bare concept of grace from her works but to present both her em-
phases on specific elements of the grace-event and the subtle nu-
ances and even discrepancies found within the total corpus of her
work. The Christian tradition has presented both the nature-enhancing, ennobling elements and the diminishing, purgative aspects of supernatural grace. Similarly, Flannery O'Connor's
writings include dimensions of both. These theological implications of the depiction of grace in her writings will be the subject of our study.

Chapter One introduces the central focus of this study: the
theological implications of the depictions of grace in her fiction. We will review the criticism, introduce the basic issues,
describe the literary devices she uses to portray the grace-
event, and suggest theological categories for use in analyzing
her concepts of grace. Chapter Two examines selected short stories, showing how her use of literary devices results in the depiction of three different kinds of grace, theologically distinct
from one another. Chapter Three discusses one imaginative theme
which O'Connor wrote three times, demonstrating that each version
depicts a theologically different concept of grace. The final
chapter examines two limit stories which reveal the depth of
O'Connor's interest in the various concepts of grace and the extent to which she sought to portray a whole spectrum of literary
representations of grace.

No adequate analysis of Flannery O'Connor's literary theology of grace has yet been written. Though some critics have
attempted to study this issue, the approach used has been
largely limited to an examination of external elements of theme
and plot which are explicitly "religious," and ignores the more
significant underlying structural processes through which
O'Connor represents the action of grace in her fiction. This
kind of analysis overlooks the range of types of grace depictions which O'Connor creations. The present study rather ana-
lyzes the literary devices found in O'Connor's narratives and
the varying modes in which they are developed and combined to
depict the various actions of grace. Our study will demonstrate
that Flannery O'Connor's fiction is not limited to a single approach to the theology of grace. Rather, she creates several
different presentations of grace, literary depictions which are
analogous to differing theologies of grace. In this way she
describes in her art the many ways in which God works in human
history.

CHAPTER ONE
THE PROBLEM OF GRACE
IN FLANNERY O'CONNOR'S FICTION

The focus of our study is the theology of grace presented in Flannery O'Connor's novels and short stories.[1] In subsequent chapters we will investigate selected narratives to describe and analyze O'Connor's depictions of the actions of grace and their theological implications. It is the purpose of this chapter to introduce the problem: first, by a brief review of the criticism of O'Connor's religious themes in general and of her portrayals of grace in particular; second, by an introduction to the problem of the depiction of grace in her fiction as something "totally unexpected yet totally believable;" third, by an analysis of the literary devices which O'Connor uses to represent the actions of grace; and fourth, by the introduction of the theological categories of grace which we will use in our later discussion.

The Relevant Criticism

To date, no adequate study of Flannery O'Connor's representations of grace has been written. Her preoccupation with grace, that is, with the active presence of God in the world of nature and persons, which she says forms the central aesthetic insight and theme in her fiction, has confused and confounded most of her critics.

Literary critics have, on the whole, sought to classify and interpret her works according to traditional categories within

---

[1]We will not here attempt to consider the theological insights expressed by O'Connor in her non-fiction writings. Whereas these theoretical statements certainly merit extended consideration, this cannot be our purpose here.

their discipline: realistic or surrealistic;[2] Southern gothic (as
typified by Edgar Allen Poe) or grotesque (also termed "neo-goth-
ic" and typified by William Faulkner);[3] or, failing this, to
identify O'Connor's fiction with that of Eudora Welty and Erskine
Caldwell.[4]

---

[2]Among the articles and reviews which assert that O'Connor
is a realist are "Review of *Wise Blood*," *United States Quarterly
Review*, 1952; Stallings, "Young Writer with a Bizarre Tale to
Tell," 1952; "Review of *A Good Man Is Hard to Find*," *Bookmark*,
1955; Gordon, "With a Glitter of Evil," 1955; Hughes, "Review of
A Good Man Is Hard to Find," 1955; Stallings, "Flannery O'Connor:
A New Shining Talent Among Our Storytellers," 1955; and Donner,
"She Writes Powerful Fiction," 1961.

Significant among those who suggest that O'Connor is a sur-
realist are Lewis, "Eccentrics' Pilgrimage," 1953; and Praz,
"Racconti del Sud," 1956.

Critics who view O'Connor as a realist, given to the frequent use of surrealistic elements, offer a variety of explana-
tions: the "strange and erratic" personality of the author herself; her interest in madness and psychosis; and the extraordinary character and concerns indigenous to the inhabitants of the
region in which O'Connor lived and about which she wrote. See,
for example, Goyen, "Unending Vengeance," 1952; "Grave and Gay:
A Review of *Wise Blood*," 1955; Nyren, "Review of *The Violent Bear
It Away*," 1960; Daniel, "A Good Writer Must Set His Book in a Region Which Is Familiar," 1960; and Mizener, "Some Kinds of Modern
Novel," 1961.

[3]Among those who consider O'Connor's work as Southern gothic
are Adams, "Fiction Chronicle," 1956; Hart, "Strange Earth, the
Stories of Flannery O'Connor," 1958; Fiedler, *Love and Death in
the American Novel*, 1960, pp. 449-451; and Hicks, "Southern Gothic with a Vengeance," 1960. For a more recent work which seeks
to link the grotesque and Christian aspects of O'Connor's work
see Schloss, *Flannery O'Connor's Dark Comedies: The Limits of In-
ference*, 1980.

Critics apply the category of "grotesque" particularly to
O'Connor's second novel: "Review of *The Violent Bear It Away*,"
Booklist, 1960; Mercier, "Sex, Success and Salvation," 1960; Ro-
senberger, "In a Bizarre Backcountry," 1960; Schott, "The Strug-
gle of Ideals is Reality," 1960; and William Van O'Connor, "The
Grotesque: An American Genre," 1962, pp. 3-19.

[4]For comparisons with Welty see, for example, Bornhauser,
"Review of *A Good Man Is Hard to Find* and *The Bride of the Innis-
fallen*," 1955; Carter, "Rhetoric and Southern Landscape," 1955;
Elder, "That Region," 1955; Hicks, "Living with Books," 1955; and
Rubin, "Two Ladies of the South," 1955. For a comparison with
Caldwell see, for example, Wylie, "The Unscented South," 1955.

The early criticism, written primarily during the fifties by literary critics and typified by concern to identify O'Connor's works according to genre and place within the Southern literary tradition, gave way in the sixties to a recognition of the religious character of her art. Some literary critics and popular religious writers began to consider her position as a Catholic writer in the Protestant fundamentalist South and the "Christian" elements of her stories and novels. This was due in part to the publication of Flannery O'Connor's new "Introduction" to the second edition of *Wise Blood* (1962), in which she briefly described her Christian viewpoint; to the increasing availability of her essays and lecture materials,[5] in which she attempted to develop a literary theology and emphasized the role of the artist as believer; to the tendency of critics to read the available fictional works in conjunction with one another, which reading revealed the religious material in her art to be neither accidental nor incidental, but central; and to the general trend of growing interest in religious writers and themes. The plethora of secondary materials written during the sixties, however, did little to resolve earlier questions and added greatly to the general confusion and misreading of O'Connor's works. Categories for making critical judgments had not been identified and divergent opinions were not adjudicated.

Flannery O'Connor's art was compared in this decade to that of Kafka, C. S. Lewis, T. S. Eliot, Bernanos, Mauriac, Flaubert, J. F. Powers, Nathaniel West, Dante, and Sophocles.[6] While there

---

[5]O'Connor published "The Fiction Writer and His Country" and "The Church and the Fiction Writer" in 1957, "The Novelist and Free Will" in 1961, and "The Role of the Catholic Novelist" in 1964. These have been republished in *Mystery and Manners*.

[6]See, for example, Pryce-Jones, "A Poignant Knowledge of the Dark," 1965; Thomas Quinn, "Lewis and O'Connor: Prophets of the Added Dimension," 1967; Robert Fitzgerald, "Introduction," in *Everything That Rises Must Converge*, 1965; Brodin, *Présences contemporaines*, 1964; Gordon, "Heresy in Dixie," 1968; Bernetta Quinn, "View from a Rock: The Fiction of Flannery O'Connor and J. F. Powers," 1958; Hawkes, "John Hawkes: An Interview," 1965; Montgomery, "Flannery O'Connor and the Natural Man," 1968; and

was nearly universal agreement that O'Connor's art proposed to
make a religious statement, there was no concurrence regarding
the nature of the statement. In part, the problem of adequate
criticism resided in the critics' inability to judge whether the
work was comedy or tragedy and whether it was to be read literally or ironically. Those favoring an ironic or comic reading
tended to see O'Connor as a secular humanist or an existentialist.[7] Those who read the works as tragicomedy tended to see
O'Connor as a Christian humanist, as an orthodox believer (either
in Christianity in general or in Roman Catholicism) or as a
Christian existentialist.[8] Few critics in the sixties understood

---

Merton, "Flannery O'Connor: A Tribute," 1964.

[7]Among those critics who propose a secular humanist or liberal interpretation are Duhamel, "Flannery O'Connor: A Tribute,"
1964; Lawson, "The Grotesque in Recent Southern Fiction," 1967;
Engle, "Insight, Richness, Humor, and Chills," 1960; Kathleen
Sullivan, "Review of *The Violent Bear It Away*," 1960; and Bliven,
"Review of *Everything That Rises Must Converge*," 1965. Among
those critics who see O'Connor as an existentialist for whom the
world is absurd are Degnan, "Review of *Everything That Rises Must
Converge*," 1965; LeClezio, "L'Univers de Flannery O'Connor," 1965;
and Stone, *Voices of Despair: Four Motifs in American Literature*,
1966, pp. 199-200, 214.

[8]A major portion of the criticism of the sixties applies one
of these labels to O'Connor's work with little discrimination.
In many instances the articles are superficial, reflecting more of
the critic's prejudices than O'Connor's art. In other instances
there is no distinction between the fact of O'Connor's personal
faith commitment and the actual portrayal of theological themes
in her fiction. Again, amid these non-critical articles, no consensus emerges. Among the critics who view O'Connor as a Christian humanist are McCown, "Flannery O'Connor and the Reality of
Sin," 1959; Ferris, "The Outside and the Inside: Flannery O'Connor's *The Violent Bear It Away*," 1960; Cheney, "Flannery O'Connor's Campaign for Her Country," 1964; Walter Sullivan, "Flannery O'Connor, Sin and Grace: *Everything That Rises Must Converge*," 1965; and Walter Sullivan, "The Achievement of Flannery
O'Connor," 1968. Among those who see O'Connor as a writer of
Christian orthodoxy are Drake, "Miss O'Connor and the Scandal of
Redemption," 1960; Drake, "The Harrowing Evangel of Flannery
O'Connor," 1964; William Van O'Connor, "Flannery O'Connor: A
Tribute," 1964; and Spivey, "Flannery O'Connor: Georgia's Theo-
logical Storyteller, 1968. The positions taken by critics re-
garding O'Connor's Catholicism will be noted later. Those

O'Connor's works to be tragedies:[9] classical, modern or Christian.

Those critics writing in the sixties who assessed Flannery O'Connor's work from the perspective of Roman Catholicism, either because of the "Catholic elements" within the fiction itself or because of O'Connor's own faith stance, found no more basis for agreement in interpretation than did those previously noted. Many of these critics judged O'Connor's work to reflect an orthodox Catholic position; some believed her stories to be a polemical statement against spiritual distortions found in the Protestant fundamentalism of the South; some viewed her art as sympathetic toward Southern evangelism in such a way as to place O'Connor among the first American ecumenical fiction writers; and others saw O'Connor as a key member of a new Catholic wing of Southern writers who had potential to create a literary renaissance in the South.[10]

---

believing O'Connor's works to be those of a Christian existentialist include Merton, "The Other Side of Despair: Notes on Christian Existentialism," 1965; and Montgomery, "Flannery O'Connor and the Natural Man," 1968.

[9]See, for example, Gardiner, "A Tragic New Image of Man," 1960; Robert Fitzgerald, "The Countryside and the True Country," 1962; Geher, "Flannery O'Connor," 1968; and Ferris, "The Outside and the Inside: Flannery O'Connor's *The Violent Bear It Away*," 1960.

[10]Among those critics who assert O'Connor's orthodoxy are Bede Sullivan, "Prophet in the Wilderness," 1960; and Stelzmann, "Shock and Orthodoxy: An Interpretation of Flannery O'Connor's Novels and Stories," 1964. Among those who hold that O'Connor seeks to attack Southern evangelism are Hunter, "Review of *The Violent Bear It Away*," 1960; and Holman, "Her Rue with a Difference," 1966. Among those stressing O'Connor's sympathy for Southern fundamentalism are Mayhew, "Flannery O'Connor's People: Authentic and Universal," 1965; and Walston, "Flannery O'Connor," 1965. An ecumenical interpretation is presented by Gable, "Ecumenic Core in Flannery O'Connor's Fiction," 1964; and Taillefer, "A Memoir of Flannery O'Connor," 1964. Hope for a rebirth in the South through the writings of Roman Catholics, especially O'Connor, is voiced by Bradbury, *Renaissance in the South*, 1964, pp. 123-124; Sessions, "Flannery O'Connor: A Memoir," 1964; and Rubin, "Southerners and Jews," 1966.

The third decade[11] of O'Connor criticism, the seventies, has
seen the publication of *The Complete Stories of Flannery O'Connor*
(1971) and a volume of her selected essays, *Mystery and Manners*
(1970). Although there is as yet no complete biography of Flannery O'Connor,[12] a brief review of her life and a list of her library holdings has recently been published,[13] as well as a collection of her letters.[14] The availability of the complete fiction corpus and of a significant number of her essays and lec-
tures, previously found only individually in scattered periodi-
cals, has provided further primary sources for scholars. Previous to this, there had been little secondary material of significant length. In 1966, Friedman and Lawson published *The Added
Dimension: The Art and Mind of Flannery O'Connor*, which was the
first collection of articles on her work, and Drake and Hyman
both brought out pamphlets surveying her life and works. In 1968,
Martin published the first volume of criticism by a single scholar.[15] Subsequent literary theologians including Browning, Eggenschwiler, Feeley and May have published full-length studies.
Although none of these volumes addresses itself specifically to
O'Connor's portrayal of grace, they represent diverse and per-
plexing assessments of her theology in general. Often her work
is judged to be orthodox (or "Thomistic") or Teilhardian,[16] and

---

[11]Clearly this categorization of secondary material according to ten-year periods is only approximate and heuristic.

[12]Sally Fitzgerald is currently working on an "official" biography.

[13]See my *Flannery O'Connor: Her Life, Library and Book Reviews*.

[14]See *The Habit of Being*, edited by Sally Fitzgerald.

[15]*The True Country: Themes in the Fiction of Flannery O'Connor*.

[16]For orthodox assessments, Christian and Roman Catholic,
see Spivey, "Flannery O'Connor: Georgia's Theological Storytel-
ler," 1968; Spivey, "Flannery O'Connor's South: Don Quixote Rides
Again," 1972; Kazin, *Bright Book of Life: American Novelists and
Storytellers from Hemingway to Mailer*, 1973, pp. 24, 34; and
Browning, *Flannery O'Connor*, 1974. Critics who believe O'Connor

some critics claim it to be ecumenical or mystical,[17] but others
suggest that it is essentially Augustinian, Jansenistic, dualist,
reductionist, or even demonic.[18]

To illustrate the diversity of views, we may compare the interpretation of Flannery O'Connor's two novels, *Wise Blood* and *The
Violent Bear It Away*. Hendin observes that much of the action in
the novels, especially in *Wise Blood*, entails violence which
leads to hopelessness on the part of the protagonist.[19] Hendin's

---

to be influenced by Teilhard de Chardin include Kann, "Everything
That Rises Must Converge," 1966; Lensing, "De Chardin's Ideas in
Flannery O'Connor," 1966; Maida, "'Convergence' in Flannery O'Con-
nor's 'Everything That Rises Must Converge,'" 1970; Flores-Del
Prado, "Flannery O'Connor's Gallery of Freaks," 1971; and Desmond,
"The Lessons of History: Flannery O'Connor's 'Everything That
Rises Must Converge,'" 1972.

[17]Critics who assert O'Connor's theology to be ecumenical
include Gable, "Ecumenic Core in Flannery O'Connor's Fiction,"
1964; Flores-Del Prado, "Flannery O'Connor's Gallery of Freaks,"
1971; and Feeley, *Voice of the Peacock*, 1972. Critics who view
O'Connor's work as essentially mystical or ascetical include
Hoobler, "Review of *Everything That Rises Must Converge*," 1965;
Hyman, *Flannery O'Connor*, 1966; and Gordon, "Heresy in Dixie,"
1968.

[18]Critics who view O'Connor's work as Augustinian include
Marks, "Advertisements for Grace: Flannery O'Connor's 'A Good
Man Is Hard to Find,'" 1966; Smith (Oates), "Ritual and Violence
in Flannery O'Connor," 1966; Thomas Quinn, "Lewis and O'Connor:
Prophets of the Added Dimension," 1967; Oates, "The Visionary Art
of Flannery O'Connor," 1973; and Millichap, "The Pauline 'Old
Man' in Flannery O'Connor's 'The Comforts of Home,'" 1974. Those
who view the narratives as Jansenistic include Allen Tate, "Flannery O'Connor: A Tribute," 1964; Coffey, "Flannery O'Connor,"
1965; Kellogg, *The Vital Tradition: The Catholic Novel in a Period of Convergence*, 1970, pp. 2, 26; McCullagh, "Aspects of Jansenism in Flannery O'Connor's *Wise Blood*," 1972; and Mellard,
"Violence and Belief in Mauriac and O'Connor," 1974. Critics
viewing O'Connor's work as dualistic include Hyman, "Flannery
O'Connor's Tattooed Christ," 1965; Hyman, *Flannery O'Connor*,
1966; and Shear, "Flannery O'Connor . . . Character and Charac-
terization," 1968. Hendin, *World of O'Connor*, argues that O'Connor's fiction is reductionist. Included among critics who view
O'Connor's fiction as demonic, if "mildly" or "unconsciously" so,
are Hawkes, "Flannery O'Connor's Devil," 1962; Rosenfield, "The
Shadow Within: The Conscious and Unconscious Use of the Double,"
1963; and Walters, *Flannery O'Connor*, 1973.

[19]Hendin, *World of O'Connor*, especially pp. 18-19, 24, 43,
60-61, and 151.

critique provides an accurate assessment of the first part of the
redemption process as O'Connor portrays it in this work. However,
Hendin does not pursue the drama of the grace-event through to
its conclusion in the work, nor does she realize that the action
of grace is not always portrayed in the same way throughout the
O'Connor corpus. In her discussion of both of the novels, Hendin
asserts that they lack any transcendent quality whatever. Thus
she concludes that O'Connor's fictional world depicts the reduc-
tion and destruction of humankind's spiritual possibility through
the engulfing action of material forces.

Eggenschwiler, on the other hand, argues that O'Connor's
novels present a Christian Humanist position. Unmindful of the
extreme reductionism noted by Hendin, which we suggest entails
an emphasis on the first portion of the grace-event as O'Connor
depicts it in both of the novels, Eggenschwiler focuses on the
transformative second portion of the narrative. He mentions *Wise
Blood* only briefly and centers his attention on the Eucharistic
references in *The Violent Bear It Away*.[20] Whereas both of these
critics offer some instructive insights, neither presents a complete view of the work from a theological perspective.

Critical opinion concerning the general quality and theological importance of the two short story collections is nearly
unanimous in its lavish praise of the author's accomplishments in
both literary execution and religious vision. Few critics have
directly compared the two works to one another. One critic who
has done so is Rubin, who believes the second volume to be inferior because of its religious overemphasis and didacticism.[21]
Another critic contends that this second work is superior precisely due to O'Connor's greater emphasis on the religious and her

---

[20]Eggenschwiler, *The Christian Humanism of Flannery O'Connor*, Chapter Three, especially pp. 114-115 and 139-140.

[21]Rubin, *The Curious Death of the Novel*, p. 265. Rubin
notes, for example, that Julian in "Everything That Rises" is so
despicable that we are unable to feel empathy for his plight,
whereas, by contrast, the Grandmother in "A Good Man Is Hard to
Find" displays a moment of genuine compassion and love.

more developed skill in "rendering so moving a portrait of man's relation to God in a secular age." [22] Although there has not yet developed a body of critical theological commentary, many who seek to contend with the religious content of these stories understand the first collection to be "negative" or "Augustinian," concentrating on the fall of humankind, our continuing sinfulness in rejecting God's grace and the power of evil in the world, and the second collection to be more "positive," even Teilhardian, reaffirming God's love of the world, the essentially sacramental nature of the universe and the inscrutability of God's will.

One critic posits the linear development of O'Connor's theology of grace from original sin (*A Good Man Is Hard to Find*) to redemption in Christ (*Everything That Rises Must Converge*). He suggests that the first collection, *A Good Man Is Hard to Find*, is influenced by O'Connor's early illness, which he believes to be the source of her desire to "battle goodness," and that the second volume, *Everything That Rises Must Converge*, is more optimistic due at least in part to the remission of her illness in confluence with her reading of Teilhard de Chardin and liberalizing changes in the Catholic Church.[23] Other critics who propose a somewhat less linear and simplistic theory, but nonetheless one based essentially on a development of O'Connor's theology of grace from an emphasis on sin, evil and the devil to one more centered in Christ, sacramentalism and positive redemption, tend to interpret the titles of the two collections literally and definitively.[24]

Among scholars who attempt an analysis of Flannery O'Connor's theology of grace, conclusions vary widely. Her concept of grace is characterized varyingly as Thomist, as Augustinian, as Jansenist—in short as representative of differing theological

---

[22]Phillips, "The Descent of the Dove," p. 54.

[23]Kirkland, "Flannery O'Connor, the Person and the Writer," pp. 159-163.

[24]See, for example, Martin, *True Country*, 1968; Driskell and Brittain, *The Eternal Crossroads: The Art of Flannery O'Connor*, 1971; and McFarland, *Flannery O'Connor*, 1976.

positions.[25] With such divergent opinion, how can O'Connor be
said to have a theology of grace at all? Is it perhaps the case
that there is no grace in her works; or that if there is grace in
her stories, its nature is such that it is not easily identifi-
able as a Christian notion of grace; or that O'Connor does not
have a single theology of grace, but more than one?

Certain critics have attempted in some detail to describe
O'Connor's theology of grace. Their purpose is to discover the
major premises and literary method of her fictional writings.
Yet none have actually analyzed the operations of grace either
theologically or functionally within the narratives. For example,
some critics interpret O'Connor's depiction of grace as Thomistic
or humanist. But the basis of this interpretation is not so much
the operation of grace in the stories as it is O'Connor's references to religious themes and motifs. Thus Martin does not examine how grace functions within a narrative so that this grace
might with some justification be called Thomistic, but rather
discusses O'Connor's thematic references to sacramentalism and
redemption.[26] Likewise Eggenschwiler, who calls O'Connor a
"Christian humanist," bases his evaluation on thematic centers
within the fiction rather than on any examination of the mode of
operation depicted in the principle of grace.[27] Both of these
critics tend to emphasize certain of O'Connor's stories over others and the short stories in general over the novels.

---

[25]We will return to these categories later in this chapter.
For the moment we need merely note that critics have generally
approached the question from a "Western" perspective, that is,
from the issue area of the nature-grace problematic, using Western schools and scholars to categorize their analysis. O'Connor
herself considered her position to be Thomist. As we will note
in more detail later, categories such as Jansenist, Augustinian,
and Thomistic, while lacking complete speculative and systematic
precision, are helpful in suggesting a spectrum of analysis analogous to O'Connor's various depictions of the actions of grace.

[26]Martin, *True Country*. See also Fitzgerald, "Assumption
and Experience: Flannery O'Connor's 'A Temple of the Holy Ghost.'"

[27]See his *Christian Humanism*, especially the "Introduction,"
pp. 9-30.

On the other hand, critics who consider O'Connor's concept of grace to be Augustinian, or even Jansenistic, tend to stress the presence of evil and violence[28] within the narratives. On this evidence and such incidental elements as Hazel Motes' negative experience with sexuality in *Wise Blood*,[29] they proclaim their theological judgments. These critics tend to emphasize the novels rather than the short stories. Hendin, whose position is even more extreme, in that she suggests that there is no grace at all in O'Connor's fiction, chooses to omit completely such seemingly "graced" stories as "The Artificial Nigger."[30]

Clearly no consensus has been reached and much of the opinion is based on subjective or naive theories. This is most frequent in the case of those critics who have enjoyed access to Flannery O'Connor's personal papers and holdings.[31] Many of these critics presume either that a literal and direct connection can be established between what O'Connor read and what she wrote[32] or that her own statements of purpose are the key to interpreting her fiction. To date, then, despite their access to new materials and their more detailed and analytic attention to the theological aspects of O'Connor's works, the critics of the seventies have produced no truly adequate analysis of her theology of grace.[33]

---

[28]See, for example, Hyman, *Flannery O'Connor*; and Walters, *Flannery O'Connor*.

[29]See McCullagh, "Aspects of Jansenism," pp. 12-16; and Asals, *Flannery O'Connor: The Imagination of Extremity*.

[30]*World of O'Connor* includes no mention, even in the Index, of this story.

[31]O'Connor's personal library holdings are eclectic, and discovery of significant themes or influences is improbable, as my own research in the Flannery O'Connor Collection at Georgia State College has confirmed. In addition, it is problematic at best to determine the extent to which a person may have been shaped by the books he or she possessed. For a complete listing of O'Connor's known holdings, see Getz, *Flannery O'Connor: Her Life, Library and Book Reviews*, pp. 85-117.

[32]The most blatant attempt is Feeley, *Voice of the Peacock*, 1972.

[33]Much of the criticism addressed to the theological implications of O'Connor's work is quite incomplete, even inaccurate,

The Problem of Grace in Flannery O'Connor

Flannery O'Connor was convinced that the description of the workings of grace is of central significance in her writings. She states that "there is a moment in every great story in which the presence of grace can be felt as it waits to be accepted or rejected, even though the reader may not recognize the moment."[34] Speaking from her own experience as a fiction writer, O'Connor explains:

> Story-writers are always thinking about what makes a story "work." From my own experience in trying to make stories "work," I have discovered that what is needed is an action that is *totally unexpected, yet totally believable*, and I have found that for me, this is always an action which indicates that grace has been offered. And frequently it is an action in which the devil has been the unwilling instrument of grace. This is not a piece of knowledge that I consciously put into my stories; it is a discovery that I get out of them.
>
> I have found, in short, from reading my own writing, that *my subject in fiction is the action of grace in territory held largely by the devil.*[35]

According to her own account, the "working" of Flannery O'Connor's stories depends upon an action that is totally unexpected. She describes this action theologically, that is, as an "action of grace in territory held largely by the devil." She could have explained the occurrence of wholly gratuitous or wholly contingent events without conveying or presenting these as "actions of grace." In contemporary literature there are many authors who describe *gratuitous* events, that is, events which arise after all adequate motivations, psychology and situations have

---

from the theological perspective. Critics often use conflicting categories with no attempt even at a description of their meaning. Some critics also demonstrate factual errors which detract from their value for the theologian of literature and suggest the inadequacy of their theological preparation for the task. McFarland, to cite one particularly bad example, continuously cites Otto Rank as the author of *The Idea of the Holy*, presumably because it was the first "Otto" that came to mind (*Flannery O'Connor*, pp. 73-89).

[34] *Mystery and Manners*, p. 118.

[35] *Mystery and Manners*, p. 118, emphasis mine.

been exhausted. For example the "mystery story" explores this boundary situation. But they do not describe or interpret these unexpected gratuitous happenings as "actions of grace," that is, as workings of God in the world. That Flannery O'Connor does seek to present such uncaused and unmerited interventions as actions of divine grace evidences her Christian theological concerns. She holds certain beliefs about the interaction between God and human persons, and these understandings inform her fiction.

O'Connor claims that the action of grace is not something which she consciously creates in her stories; rather she discovers it there. This description, although appealing in its reliance on spontaneity and "gratuity," fails to recognize that, as author, O'Connor herself creates the devilish territory which her characters inhabit and the plots which constitute her stories. Though the grace-event may be unexpected from the perspective of the character or the plot, and though O'Connor may attempt to suggest that in "real life" such grace-events are equally unexpected, she nonetheless creates them and their contexts, and so she must be held responsible for their nature and their meaning in her stories. It is thus possible and, indeed, necessary for a theologian of literature to ask, despite Flannery O'Connor's protestation of discovery rather than creativity, how exactly she does compose these situations and events. What theological meaning is conveyed *by the way in which* O'Connor contextualizes the events she sees as "grace-filled" and the responses her characters make to them?

A central question, therefore, is that of the "totally-unexpected-yet-totally-believable" characteristic of the action of grace in Flannery O'Connor's stories. The question can be approached from both a literary and a theological point of view, and the theologian of literature must attempt to grasp this combined perspective. From the literary perspective, we must discover the literary devices by which O'Connor creates a grace-event which can then be discovered to be *both* unexpected and believable. A believable event is, from the point of view of the

reader, one that is anticipated, reasonable, even looked forward
to with confidence. On the other hand, an unexpected event is,
from the point of view of the reader, one that is sudden, amazing
and unanticipated--an unforeseeable contingency. In creating
"grace-events" in her stories, Flannery O'Connor seeks to create
events that are *both* believable and unexpected. The key is that
something contingent must occur which, although interpreted as
contingent can also be interpreted by the reader as believable
in retrospect. That is, the "grace-event" reveals to the reader
(and sometimes also to the story's protagonist) that there is a
deeper order of intentionality and development pervading the entire narrative that the reader is now able to recognize.

The terms "unexpected" and "believable" both refer to the
literal or "natural" level of the story. That is, Flannery O'Connor describes her task as the depiction of events which on the natural literal level are not fully caused, yet which are on that
same level totally believable. She does not create events which
are miraculous in the extreme *deus ex machina* sense, events which
could empirically be described only as direct interventions and
contradictions of the laws of physical nature. Yet O'Connor intends these actions of grace to be characterized by a quality
which, while not strictly miraculous, renders them at least surprising, even paradoxical. This quality she characterizes as
"unexpected." The unexpected and believable aspects of the workings of grace operate on the natural level, but against the as-
sumptions of the reader. The resulting paradox indicates the
presence of something "more," something mysterious, wonderful and
gratuitous--grace--the supernatural element which resolves or
illuminates the startling, paradoxical situation she has created.

O'Connor combines elements in her stories which are ordinar-
ily considered to be contraries. That is the core of her artist-
ry in the creation of the moment which she calls "grace." By
uniting the aspects "unexpected" and "believable," Flannery
O'Connor is undertaking the task of the author as literary theologian.

The fiction writer, like the theologian, must create a larger

universe of discourse within which something totally unexpected
can yet be totally believable. O'Connor states that the action
or gesture which is *both totally right and totally unexpected*
"has to be one that is both in character and beyond character; it
has to suggest both the world and eternity."[36] For the fiction
writer, then, unlike the theologian, the "larger universe of
meaning and discourse" is not a higher level of abstraction and
systematic definition. Whereas the theologian may speak of
"levels" and may define acts as if they were unambiguous references, the novelist or short story writer must work within the
limits of the narrative itself. It must be something *within* the
story--a certain working of literary materials--that provides
the larger parameters of meaning within which something totally
unexpected becomes believable to the reader. Moreover, many of
Flannery O'Connor's stories focus on conversion and salvation of
her characters so that the unexpected change in these characters
will somehow be perceived as a believable, though surprising *act
of grace*. This is the form of irony of her conversion accounts.

An act of grace must be portrayed as some action or gesture
which is *totally right* or appropriate to insure its believability
and yet it must also be *totally unexpected* in order to suggest
its gratuitous divine origin. According to O'Connor, such an action or gesture would transcend allegorical and moral categories
because of its contact with *mystery*.[37] In other words, Flannery
O'Connor believes that grace, which she understands as the heart
of a story, must be depicted at once as mysterious and divine,
yet intimately related to character and plot. It must be both
"in character" and "beyond character." The surface level and
mysterious level must each be adequately portrayed by the fiction
writer. For O'Connor, who believes that life is essentially mysterious, those aspects of natural life which are presented and
accentuated are those which most directly enable the writer to
describe human life to its own limit. That is, O'Connor is

---

[36]*Mystery and Manners*, p. 111.

[37]*Mystery and Manners*, p. 111.

essentially interested in the boundary situation where humanity
reaches out toward the mystery that lies "beyond character" and
beyond nature. It is at this point that the supernatural possibilities of life become manifest. She says:

> . . . if the writer believes that our life is and will
> remain essentially mysterious, if he looks upon us as
> beings existing in a created order to whose laws we
> freely respond, then what he sees on the surface will be
> of interest to him only as he can go through it into an
> experience of mystery itself. His kind of fiction will
> always be pushing its own limits outward toward the
> limits of mystery, because for this kind of writer, *the
> meaning of a story does not begin except at a depth where
> adequate motivation and adequate psychology and the var-
> ious determinations have been exhausted.*[38]

For a writer such as Flannery O'Connor who is interested in
the mystery of life, it is precisely what we do not easily understand that is captivating and fruitful.

> Such a writer will be interested in what we don't under-
> stand rather than in probability. He will be interested
> in characters who are forced out to meet evil and grace
> and who act on a trust beyond themselves--whether they
> know very clearly what it is they act upon or not.[39]

The key in this description is O'Connor's statement that
"the meaning of the story does not begin except at a depth where
adequate motivation and adequate psychology and the various de-
terminations have been exhausted." That is to say, after all
the natural causes and possibilities for action have been explored and used up, the action still goes on. The action continues unexpectedly because there is no adequate motivation,
psychology or determination. It goes on because there is something mysteriously more in the universe that impinges upon our
lives when all the natural and understandable possibilities for
action have been exhausted. There is an unanticipatable or
transnatural possibility that can be seen, even described, once
the natural possibilities have been used up.

Describing how these natural possibilities are exhausted so

---

[38]*Mystery and Manners*, pp. 41-42, emphasis mine.

[39]*Mystery and Manners*, p. 42.

that (or until) this mysterious higher possibility appears is, according to Flannery O'Connor, the task of the author. The writer accomplishes this by utilizing the devices of authorship. That is, as author creating character, plot or situation, she uses "the tricks of the trade." The author cannot merely evoke mystery by incantation. She is not a priest. She uses language, and in this case must use language to create a world which is limited yet open to mystery. She must create actions that exceed motivations and the natural possibilities of character. To do this she makes use of certain literary devices.

Literary Devices and Types of Grace

In the first part of this chapter we noted that most of the critical writing concerning Flannery O'Connor's theology of grace limits its data to the thematic and specifically "religious" elements in her fiction, ignoring the more essential aspects of the method and process by which she develops her differing portrayals of grace. That is, the critics we have noted emphasize religious elements and themes, and attempt on that basis to distinguish O'Connor's theology of grace as Thomistic, Jansenistic, heretical, and so on. This is insufficient. Our purpose here is to go beyond this to describe how the very *process* by which O'Connor conceives and develops her narratives determines the type of grace which characterizes each work.

More than the mere external "element" (the presence of a prophet, the Eucharist, God-language) is involved in creating these distinct depictions of grace. Rather it is the very way in which Flannery O'Connor uses literary devices to create and control her stories that determines the distinctions among her approaches to grace. A detailed study of these devices and their modalities of application, modalities which lead to portrayals of different concepts of grace, will be the focus of our study in the following chapters. In this section we will introduce some of the literary devices which O'Connor uses and give a general description of how each is employed to portray the various types of grace which she presents.[40]

In order to accomplish her purpose in fiction, namely, to portray in short story or novel form the "action of grace in a territory held largely by the devil," Flannery O'Connor--like any author--employs certain literary devices. Among these are (1) the multivalent symbol, (2) discrepancy in action between intention and outcome, and (3) moment of recognition.[41] By

---

[40]Further clarification of the complexities introduced here will be made in subsequent chapters, when our discussion of specific narratives will help by giving detailed examples of how O'Connor uses these literary devices.

[41]I am indebted to Northrop Frye for assistance in developing and discussing these literary devices for analyzing O'Connor's work. For further consideration of these and similar literary techniques, see Frye, *The Secular Scripture: A Study in the Structure of Romance*, pp. 36ff. on displacement as a device for making the "impossible probable"; pp. 46ff. on coincidence and the vertical perspective; pp. 130ff. on recognition as a means of character transformation; pp. 140ff. on reversal and metamorphosis, and pp. 151ff. on multivalent symbols; also Frye, *Anatomy of Criticism: Four Essays*, pp. 71-128 on multivalent symbols; pp. 136-138 on displacement. Aristotle, in the *Poetics*, discusses two of these three devices. What we have called discrepancy in action he calls peripety or reversal. He gives definitions: "A reversal is a change . . . by which the action veers around in the opposite direction . . . in accordance with the laws of probability or necessity . . . [and] recognition is a change by which those marked (by the plot) for good or for bad fortune pass from a state of ignorance into a state of knowledge . . ." (No. 11, trans. Epps, p. 21). He discusses the kinds of recognition in No. 16, but they are not relevant to our use of the device here. Symbolism as such is largely neglected, as has been noted (Solmsen, "Introduction," p. vi), though he does discuss the use of metaphor and simile. The best plots are complex ones, those which include both reversal and recognition (Nos. 10, 11). Aristotle insists on probability and decries the use of a *deus ex machina* (No. 15), insisting: "Poets should choose impossibilities which are probable rather than possibilities which are unconvincing. They should not make their plots from parts which are contrary to reason" (No. 24, trans. Epps, p. 53). He also insists that characters be probable, and not inconsistent (No. 15). Specifically, recognition must not be incredible: "Of all forms of recognition, the best is that which results from the incidents themselves in which the astonishment too results from what is probable" (No. 16, trans. Epps, p. 33). These remarks correspond to O'Connor's notion of the

skillfully utilizing these literary techniques, O'Connor is able to depict the works of grace in a manner which is "both unexpected and believable" in her fiction.

We will discuss each of the three literary devices and the various ways in which O'Connor uses them. We will discover that O'Connor utilizes each device in three unique ways, thus portraying three specific, divergent concepts of grace. Our contention is that O'Connor does not limit her depiction of grace to a single approach. Rather she presents at least three different ways in which grace operates, each of which is created by a specialized application of the literary devices of multivalent symbols, discrepancy in action between intention and outcome, and moment of recognition, used in combination with one another.

Multivalent Symbols

The first literary device through which Flannery O'Connor depicts varying concepts of grace in her fiction is that of the multivalent symbol. By this we mean that an object which has a clear and definite meaning on one level becomes meaningful in another sense and/or on another level within the narrative. In O'Connor's stories, the multivalent symbol is used to depict some action of grace, the gratuitous intervention of the supernatural into the natural development of the plot. The "moment of grace" is that moment in which the meaning of the symbol is changed or expanded. In this moment, the symbol becomes multivalent. How this occurs differs depending on the type of grace O'Connor seeks to portray. That is, the precise manner in which symbolism is employed both in itself and in conjunction with other literary techniques distinguishes the various differing presentations of grace in O'Connor's works.

In the first type of presentation of grace, a symbol which originally carries a single, limited meaning gradually attains

---

unexpected yet believable action of grace which she depicts by literary devices.

199 864

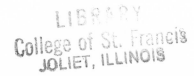

other related and implied meanings. These additional meanings
deepen and expand the original connotation of the symbol. These
further significations may even be contrary, and the moment of
grace may unite them in an unexpected convergence of opposites.
In the central moment of grace, the protagonist experiences an
insight, the revelation of the full meaning of the symbol.

In this type of symbolism, the original meaning of the symbol is extended and gains a further meaning previously unsuspected by either the protagonist or the reader. This additional
meaning points beyond the original "natural" significance of the
symbol to a further "supernatural" significance. The natural
meaning of the symbol is retained and complemented by a new,
supernatural meaning. Both meanings are confirmed in the multivalence of the symbol at the moment of grace. The "action of
grace" here entails the multivalent meanings of the natural and
supernatural at one and the same time. Through this use of symbol, grace is depicted as nature-enhancing. The original, natural symbol is enriched through the addition of supernatural
value.

A different use of symbol depicts a second concept of grace
quite different from the first. A symbol begins with two meanings which are in opposition to one another. At the moment of
grace, one meaning is rejected while the other meaning is vali-
dated through the supernatural intervention. In stories which
portray this second type of grace, the reader recognizes the two
opposing meanings from the outset of the story, while the protagonist is aware only of the natural meaning. In the light provided by the grace-event, the protagonist sees for the first time the
true, namely, the supernatural meaning. He or she must then
choose to accept or reject the reality which the newly revealed
meaning of the symbol suggests.[42] The action of grace here

---

[42]Some critics have gone to great lengths to examine which
characters seem to accept this grace in order to establish a list
of O'Connor's "saved" characters. In many cases, such a conclusion simply cannot be drawn from the plot of the story. For

centers in the enlightenment of the protagonist brought about through the distinct separation of opposite meanings contained within the original symbol.

Whereas the first type of grace employs symbols to indicate the complementary relationship between nature and grace through the enriching of the symbol, namely, the addition of a supernatural meaning to the natural meaning, the second begins with a multivalent symbol which is broken down into opposing natural and supernatural components. Through the action of grace, the natural element is upheld and confirmed as the real value.

A third type of grace is depicted through symbols in yet another way. Here the symbol itself becomes the active transformative principle in the grace-event. A symbol whose natural meaning is known to both the reader and the protagonist gradually takes on a supernatural meaning for the reader. The protagonist, who undergoes a radical change through the action of the symbol itself, gradually becomes transformed until he or she becomes identified with the new meaning of the symbol. The protagonist gradually loses his or her personal qualities through a kind of metamorphosis process. The void created in the transformation is filled by the transferred symbolic identity. According to this concept of grace, human nature is changed into a kind of supernature. The symbol generates a meaning which acts to change the identity of the protagonist. Here grace might be said to displace or transubstantiate nature. Here the natural meaning is not enriched or reversed, but displaced, that is, the natural meaning of the symbol is changed to a related, but more intense supernatural meaning.

---

further discussion of this question, together with a list of problematic endings, see May, *Pruning Word*, p. xxi. As Merton points out, O'Connor refuses to make final judgments of this kind (Merton, "Prose Elegy," pp. 41-42, see Getz, *Flannery O'Connor*, p. 51. O'Connor seems to be far more concerned to develop the "possibility" of illumination or conversion through grace than to determine the ultimate state of the characters.

Discrepancy in Action
between Intention and Outcome

A second literary device which O'Connor uses to depict various concepts of grace is discrepancy in action between intention and outcome. O'Connor creates situations in which the intended outcome of human actions is in some way changed or reversed. By these altered outcomes, O'Connor indicates the influence of a divine intention which prevails in the affairs of persons, overruling their own intentions. The humanly intended course of events is in this way uplifted, reversed or impeded by a supernatural interference.

Discrepancy in action between intention and outcome, caused by divine intervention, is also of three types. In the first way, the divine intervention enhances and ennobles the original human intention. That is, the protagonist's goal is reached, but it has been enhanced through some other turn of events, producing an outcome whose discrepancy rests in the achievement of a goal or end superior to that expected by the protagonist. Here the outcome is related to the original intention, but it is more than what was expected. Something more noble than the human intention has been added to the result.

The second way in which O'Connor employs the device of discrepancy in action between intention and outcome consists of an action which produces not the outcome intended by the protagonist, but its opposite. In these stories, the protagonist acts deliberately in order to achieve a certain natural goal. However, through an outside intervention or unexpected turn of events, representing a supernatural, opposing will, his or her original intention is thwarted and the divine intention carries the protagonist to a new, and oppostite, supernatural goal.

The third way in which O'Connor utilizes the device entails the complete stopping or cessation of the action, but not until the action has been driven beyond the intention of the protagonist. That is, a protagonist undertakes an action with a given intention. As the story develops, the action gains a momentum beyond his or her intention and control. When the action finally ceases, the protagonist has been victimized. He or she is completely incapacitated, totally displaced by grace. Now reduced to non-action, the protagonist becomes a burnt-out case, a sign for others of the power of God.

Moment of Recognition

The third literary device used by O'Connor to portray various notions of grace is the moment of recognition, the moment in the narrative in which the meaning of the story itself is revealed. The revelation is considered to be "primary" when it is the protagonist who experiences the insight and "secondary" when the meaning is given to or explained by a character who is not the protagonist, but who witnesses the experience of the protagonist. Of course, in every story there is what might be termed the "tertiary recognition," that of the reader.

In O'Connor's first use of the device, the protagonist realizes and acknowledges that he or she has received something unmerited and unexpected which uplifts or ennobles him or her. The protagonist recognizes that the "gift" or grace has a supernatural source, but does not see it to be contrary to the natural order. The main character comes to understand that his or her own actions are of positive value. In these stories, the "recognition of grace" is presented as a maturation which develops from the positive aspects of human nature and builds on the integrity of human action and willing. Something is thereby added to the protagonist; but the action of grace, an intrusion of the supernatural, does not alter his or her natural condition or destroy his or her will. Rather, it enriches and uplifts them. The protagonist has received some addition to his or her life which complements and enhances the natural condition. Usually this recognition entails some greater awareness of the goodness of God and the world. The protagonist matures spiritually by gaining a broader understanding of divine providence in his or her life.

In O'Connor's second use of the moment of recognition, the

protagonist has been forced through some violent occurrence to a
boundary situation. The recognition entails the sudden awareness
of the protagonist's helplessness in the face of a power (supernatural) greater than himself. The focus of the awareness rests
on the radical opposition between the human (natural) will and
the divine (supernatural) will. Whereas the protagonist has interpreted the symbols in his or her world in a certain way, or
initiated an action to produce a naturally desirable result, he
or she now experiences the negation and collapse of this natural
understanding of the world or of human volition in the face of a
supernatural meaning or action. The moment of recognition here
is thus the sudden awareness of the reversal of the protagonist's
earlier understanding of the situation. It is a moment of conversion, or at least of its possibilty.

Rather than being an uplifting spiritual experience or an
inclusive vision of God, this second type of recognition dis-
closes the sin and error of the protagonist. The protagonist
"recognizes" the collapse of his or her purpose and sees it to
be the result of God's intervention.

The response of O'Connor's protagonist to this call to conversion varies from story to story. In some cases the protagonist accepts the call and changes his or her life radically. In
other stories, O'Connor's protagonists are inadequate to the
power of the revelation. They may even die as a result of it.
In these stories the full meaning of the protagonist's experience
must be interpreted by the reader in a supplementary tertiary
recognition.

O'Connor's third use of recognition is characterized by the
displacement of the protagonist through the action of grace so as
to make any primary recognition impossible. In these stories, the
protagonist is not converted, but broken and destroyed. In this
type of grace-event, a secondary character, often the antagonist,
recognizes the event as grace. The secondary character sees in
the destruction of the protagonist an act of God.

O'Connor treats this kind of secondary recognition in two
different ways. In some of her stories, the secondary character

sympathizes in some manner with the changed condition of the protagonist. In other stories, however, the secondary character has
been the antagonist throughout the story. In this case, the antagonist plays a definite role in the final devastation of the
character of the protagonist. In such an event, the antagonist
presents a negative recognition of the grace-event which has
transformed the opponent. Here, the negative statement high-
lights and provides contrast to the new state of the protagonist.
The reader then participates in a tertiary recognition which includes the new condition of the protagonist and its negative
assessment through the antagonist, who is not reconciled, but
rather revealed to be ignorant in matters of spiritual transformation and the action of grace.

In summary form, we can now present Flannery O'Connor's
three differing presentations of grace:

(1) The three different uses of the multivalent symbol:
   a) harmonious reconciliation of opposites; grace with
      nature; grace builds on nature.
   b) maintained polarization; grace opposes nature.
   c) displacement; grace replaces nature.

(2) The three different uses of discrepancy in action be-
     tween intention and outcome:
   a) continuing single direction of development.
   b) reversal and counter-development.
   c) lack of continuation; broken plot and development;
      displacement of the protagonist.

(3) The three different uses of the moment of recognition:
   a) maturation; broader understanding.
   b) call to conversion; change in direction.
   c) secondary recognition only; protagonist becomes
      sign.

Stories	Symbol	Discrepancy	Recognition
Type a	harmony	continuity	maturation

| Type b | opposition | reversal | call to conver-sion |
| Type c | displacement | cessation | none (secondary) |

Theological Analogues

Flannery O'Connor's presentations of the action of grace, which utilize the literary devices we have just described, depict three different grace concepts analogous to certain Christian doctrines of grace as developed in systematic theological thought. O'Connor was a literary theologian, not a systematic theologian. She does not address many doctrinal issues raised by the systematic study of grace, such as the precise distinctions and interrelationships of election and reprobation, efficacious and merely sufficient grace, God's universal salvific will and predestination, divine foreknowledge and human freedom, and so on. Yet she does clearly present in a literary way three different understandings of the action of grace. These three representations of grace are analogous to three Christian approaches to grace attributed to the Thomistic, Augustinian and Jansenistic schools.

Thomistic Grace

We begin by recalling O'Connor's use of literary devices in their first mode. With regard to symbols in these stories, we have seen that, in the resolution of the plot, the natural meaning of the symbol is not negated, but confirmed and expanded. As the narrative unfolds, the symbols gain an additional meaning beyond the natural capabilities of the object which symbolizes it. This further meaning ennobles and uplifts nature. Within the symbol, grace completes nature. Grace here involves a growth toward a fuller maturity. This affirmation of the natural is similar to the teaching of Christian theologians who hold that grace does not negate, but perfects and expands the meaning of nature. This position asserts that the supernatural order is not opposed to but is a further, qualitatively new development of the natural order. In this type of story, therefore, Flannery O'Connor uses symbols in a way analogous to Thomism.

The use of the literary device of discrepancy in action between intention and outcome in these stories is such that the original intention is confirmed and enhanced by the operation of grace. More than what was expected in the natural order is given in the outcome of the act. The "more" is the effect of supernatural grace. Similarly, the recognition which obtains in these stories results in a broader understanding by the protagonist of the glory of God's love. The common element is that grace builds on nature, adds a qualitatively new dimension to the natural order which is not owed it, which is totally gratuitous, but which is not in opposition to or a negation of the natural elements. These characteristics of the relationship between grace and nature are those generally attributed to the Thomistic school.

Thomism, in the sense in which we refer to it here, is wider than the theology of Aquinas himself. It includes notions of nature and grace contributed by his commentators as well as theological developments flowing from his insights.[43] In many ways Thomas himself was Augustinian in his approach to grace.[44] Yet his insights on nature and grace suggest a relationship between them more harmonious than that found in Augustine.[45] For Thomas, there exists in persons a *natural* desire to see God. The created intellect naturally tends to this end.[46] Grace builds on

---

[43]Scholars distinguish "strict" from "wide" Thomism (for example, Weisheipl, "Thomism," pp. 126-127). It is the latter to which we refer.

[44]Rondet, *Grace of Christ*, pp. 213, 222, 229, 233-246; E[ugene] Burke, "Grace," pp. 661-662.

[45]Rondet holds that "thorough research would probably show that in Thomas' thought nature and grace fit together harmoniously." He adds, however, that the qualification "probably" is necessary, since the question has not been resolved (*Grace of Christ*, p. 223).

[46]Thomas Aquinas, *Summa Theologica*, I, q. 12; *Contra Gentiles*, III, 50-57. See O'Grady, *Christian Anthropology*, pp. 47-48; Rondet, *Grace of Christ*, pp. 210-211; Regan, "Grace and Nature," p. 684.

this natural desire, elevating the human person's end to the
supernatural one which is the Beatific Vision.[47] The supernatural end brings direction and consistency to the natural order.[48]
Grace is indispensable if one is to attain this now-elevated
goal.[49] Supernatural virtues, analogous to natural ones but in-
fused by the gratuitous operation of grace, are necessary for
acts leading to salvation.[50] Thus the approach Thomas uses to
the question of the operation of grace is based on an analogy to
the natural order.[51]

In general the approach to Christian grace attributed to the
Thomistic school emphasizes the harmony between nature and grace,
reason and faith.[52] The God who redeems is the God who creates.
Grace builds on nature and perfects it. In these ways, one of
O'Connor's modes of depicting grace is analogous to a Thomistic
approach to the theology of grace.[53]

Augustinian Grace

In a second type of story, Flannery O'Connor uses her literary devices in a different manner. The resolution of the plot
involves a separation and rejection of the natural meaning of the
multivalent symbol. The natural and supernatural meanings of the

---

[47]Rondet, *Grace of Christ*, pp. 214-216; Regan, "Grace and
Nature," p. 684; Weisheipl, "Thomism," p. 128.

[48]E[ugene] Burke, "Grace," p. 662.

[49]Weisheipl, "Thomism," p. 128; Regan, "Grace and Nature,"
p. 684; Rondet, *Grace of Christ*, pp. 211, 219-220.

[50]Rondet, *Grace of Christ*, pp. 220-224.

[51]E[ugene] Burke, "Grace," p. 662; Weisheipl, "Thomism," pp.
127-128.

[52]Weisheipl, "Thomism," p. 128.

[53]No attempt has been made here to unravel the inconsisten-
cies or unresolved questions either in the thought of Thomas himself or in that of his theological descendants. Questions concerning the precise relationship of nature and grace continue to
be disputed within Christianity, as their mysterious and paradoxical character necessitates. Contemporary theologians are still
probing these unresolved issues (see, for example, Rondet, *Grace
of Christ*, p. 248; O'Grady, *Christian Anthropology*, pp. 49-59).

symbols are polarized, and the opposition between them is emphasized such that, in the moment of grace, the natural meaning is
shown to belong to the order of sin. Grace opposes nature. Similarly, in this second use of discrepancy between intent and outcome, grace operates to reverse the original, natural intention
of the protagonist. The outcome is not merely *different* from
what the protagonist had intended, but the outcome is actually
contrary to the original goal. Moreover, the moment of recognition involves a call to repentance, an acknowledgment that one's
prior aspirations have been shown to be contrary to God's will.[54]
These stories are therefore analogous to an Augustinian theology
of grace.

Augustinianism, like Thomism, includes not only the teachings of the original thinker, but also the additions and commen-
taries of his theological descendants. Complete consistency cannot be expected.[55] Scholars note that certain aspects of Augustine's own thought on grace and nature have been exaggerated by
some who claim to be his followers.[56] These issues cannot concern us here. The Augustinianism to which we refer suggests a
general approach to the theology of grace and nature which describes nature as so infected and disordered by sin that the work
of grace involves, at least to a considerable extent, the rejection of nature, that is, sinful nature.

One example among many of this tendency can be seen in the
description given by Augustine of how in his early life, before
his conversion, he wept bitterly at the death of a friend, but

---

[54]Once again we must note here that O'Connor does not clearly distinguish the "saved" from the "damned." Sometimes the protagonist seems to accept the call to conversion, sometimes not;
in some cases the result is uncertain. Type b recognition always involves a realization of the *call* to conversion, of God's
insistence that the protagonist reverse direction, but does not
always include the acceptance of that call.

[55]Rondet notes that even within Augustine's own writings
there are discrepancies, and that it is necessary to "correct
Augustine with Augustine" (*Grace of Christ*, pp. 141-144).

[56]Russell, "Augustinianism," p. 1064.

how after his conversion he claims his former grief to have been
the result of unbelief, and tries to control his sorrow over
death, "for he alone loses none dear to him, to whom all are dear
in Him who cannot be lost."[57] In the view of grace typically
called Augustinian, the only right love is love for God, and all
other loves--familial, sexual, cultural, even philosophical
love of truth--are sinful tendencies of the human heart which
strives against grace.[58] In this Augustinian understanding,
therefore, grace does not confirm and uplift nature, but opposes
it.[59] Augustinianism stresses the medicinal aspects of grace and
the correlative disorder of human nature, which is in dire need
of a cure.[60] A kind of "Augustinian pessimism" has thus been
attributed to this school of thought, which is analogous to the
kind of presentation of nature and grace found in some of Flannery O'Connor's stories. It must be stressed, however, that this
"pessimism" is intended to serve as a means of access to the
grace of Christ, a kind of counterpoint which, by strongly sig-
nalling the disease from which humankind suffers, might lead it

---

[57]Augustine, *Confessions*, p. 56. When later, after his conversion, his mother Monica dies, Augustine admits some continuing sorrow, but ascribes it to the incompleteness of his conversion (p. 149).

[58]Philosophy is excluded as an autonomous endeavor and sub-
jected to the primacy of Faith (Russell, "Augustinianism," pp.
1063, 1065). Sexual love, especially, was disparaged by Augustine. Though there are scholars who defend him from charges that
he identified sexual love with concupiscence (for example, Hugo
in his *St. Augustine on Nature, Sex, and Marriage*), a reading of
the anti-Pelagian treatises, in particular, suggests that Augustine, while not totally consistent, does tend to see sexual love
as particularly disordered by original sin. The *Confessions*
themselves show this emphasis (pp. 50, 153-186, etc.).

[59]Of course, nature here is not to be interpreted in the
Thomistic sense of nature as inherently good. What is meant
rather is nature pervaded with and corrupted by sin. It is precisely this difference in emphasis in the understanding of nature
which lies at the center of the difference between these two
views of nature and grace.

[60]Russell, "Augustinianism," p. 1067; Russell, "Augustinianism, Theological School of," pp. 1069, 1071.

to seek a cure by accepting the grace of Christ which alone can
lead to salvation. The ultimate purpose of Augustine's stress on
the corruption of nature is not its destruction, but its conversion. Augustinian pessimism is eschatologically optimistic.[61]

In general, then, the Augustinian school emphasizes the opposition between fallen nature and supernatural grace. Grace
must reverse the sinful tendencies which would otherwise lead
humankind to damnation. It is this stress on the opposition between nature and grace, even though the ultimate purpose is reconciliation and salvation, which is the point of analogy to the
presentation of grace in this series of O'Connor's stories.[62]

Jansenistic Grace

A third group of stories differ significantly from both of
Flannery O'Connor's other narrative forms in that here the natural level is altogether displaced by the supernatural. Whereas
the first mode is characterized by harmonious reconciliation of
symbolic meanings, by an enhancement of the protagonist's original intention and by a recognition of this enrichment resulting
in spiritual maturation; and the second by a separation and opposition of the levels of symbolic meaning, a reversal of the

---

[61]Rondet, *Grace of Christ*, pp. 135-139. Augustine's purpose in emphasizing the disorder in nature was salvific. He accuses the Pelagians of besetting human nature with "cruel praise
. . . . For whosoever shall believe your laudation, will never
bring their babes to Christ for his salvation" (*De nuptiis et
concupiscentia*, II, 9, translation from *St. Augustine's Anti-Pelagian Works*, Vol 5 of the *Nicene and Post Nicene Fathers* series).
Similarly, in the *Confessions*, Augustine relates the story
of his sinful past as a counterpoint to the ultimately accepted
grace of Christ. In a sense, this past life retains meaning even
though the meaning is now known to be sinful and has been rejected. It has some positive value, if only as a witness to the need
of grace.

[62]In these stories, the natural meaning of the symbol and
the original intention of the protagonist, even though rejected
by grace, retain some positive value. They are used in a manner
not unlike Augustine's "confession" of his sinful past. They
point up the need for grace.

protagonist's intention and the recognition of a call to conversion; stories of this third type are characterized by a total
displacement of nature by supernature. In these stories, the
natural meaning of the symbols is eliminated in favor of a supernatural meaning. Here the discrepancy in action is such that the
natural plot development stops. The action of grace intervenes
not merely to reverse the natural development of the narrative,
but to displace it completely. There can be no continuation of
the story, since the protagonist has been burnt-out, transubstantiated by the action of grace. And there can be no primary recognition or conversion since the protagonist is no longer able to
recall his or her former state. There is no continuity of self-
hood. Following the action of grace, the protagonist is merely
a sign of God's power. These characteristics suggest an analogy
to Jansenism.

Jansenism is a particular theological understanding of nature and grace which is based not only on the original teachings
of Jansenius, but also on the expansions and applications of his
ideas made by his followers. Although some of the later developments are not in exact agreement with Jansenius' own notions,[63]
Jansenism as a school of theology and piety does suggest his general approach to the questions of grace, nature, repentance and
redemption which emphasizes the need for a severe purgation of
human nature through the action of grace.

The key notion in Jansenism is that of irresistible grace.
Jansenius took the most rigid of Augustine's concepts and accepted them without nuance, pushing them to their extremes.[64] Nature is so corrupted by sin that not only is grace necessary for
redemption, but this grace must be so strong that in his fallen

---

[63]Cognet, "Jansenism," pp. 820-824.

[64]Cognet, "Jansenism," p. 820; Burke, "Grace," p. 657; Rondet, *Grace of Christ*, pp. 340-352. The title of Jansenius'
treatise was *Augustinus*. The author believed that he was offer-
ing the only theology of grace true to Augustine (Cognet, p.
820).

state natural man cannot resist it.[65] Predestination is absolute. There is no such thing as grace offered and rejected (sufficient grace in scholastic theology), since grace, once offered, is overwhelming and must be accepted. Human freedom is thus replaced by grace.[66] From this doctrine came a piety which emphasized extreme penance as fitting for one filled with the power of grace. The natural and supernatural, material and spiritual levels were thoroughly separated from each other, and the former was to be eliminated by penance working in conjunction with the operation of grace.[67]

The points of analogy to O'Connor's third mode of stories are obvious. Grace replaces nature. The natural intention and freedom of the protagonist are displaced by the overwhelming power of divine grace. Unlike the Augustinian stories, where the natural level is seen as a counterpoint to the supernatural, as having meaning at least as a call to conversion (we noted that in the *Confessions* Augustine gave positive value even to his sinful life, in that this past sinful state was a proof of the need for Christ's grace), in the Jansenistic works the natural level is displaced, removed completely by the operations of grace. It is literally worn out or burnt-out—totally displaced by the supernatural dimension, transubstantiated into a sheer sign of God's power. The protagonist is changed from being an agent and having a personality with a will, whether sinful or graced, unconverted or converted, into becoming a sign, even an impersonal, passive object, which testifies that God alone has reality and power. The plot ends, since the protagonist can no longer act. Grace is a barrier which prevents further human action. These aspects are analogous to the Jansenistic doctrine of grace.

---

[65]Rondet, *Grace of Christ*, pp. 343-344; E[ugene] Burke, "Grace," p. 665; Cognet, "Jansenism," p. 820.

[66]Rondet, *Grace of Christ*, pp. 340-345; Cognet, "Jansenism," pp. 820-821; E[ugene] Burke, "Grace," p. 665; Aherne, "Grace," p. 667.

[67]Matteucci, "Jansenistic Piety," pp. 825-826.

CHAPTER TWO
THREE PRESENTATIONS OF GRACE

In Flannery O'Connor's fiction there is not a single concept of grace, but several different types of grace narrations. This judgment differs in two ways from that commonly offered.[1] First, many critics have based their analyses of grace in O'Connor on her inclusion of "religious elements" in various works, or on the fact that she claimed to write about the action of grace. We have noted the inadequacy of these approaches. Our own analysis is based on distinguishing among the central literary devices in the stories themselves, in order to analyze how they serve to depict the occurrence of grace within the structure of the narrative. This analysis moves beyond the conceptual content found in her fiction to the process and method of its presentation. Second, many critics have argued that O'Connor's stories give evidence of Thomism, or Augustinianism, or Jansenism, or ecumenism, or dualism, and so on. Our own analysis suggests that no one category is sufficient, since Flannery O'Connor creates specifically different types of grace narratives. There is no single approach to or theology of grace which is solely characteristic of her fiction writing. She quite clearly presents a range of approaches to grace which cannot be summarized by any one category, either literary or theological.

This chapter will be divided into three sections, each describing O'Connor's use of literary devices to portray a particular type of grace. First, we will study depictions of Thomistic grace in "A Temple of the Holy Ghost" and "The Artificial Nigger." Second, we will analyze her portrayals of Augustinian

---

[1]For an overview of the relevant criticism, see the first section of Chapter One.

grace in "Greenleaf" and "Everything That Rises Must Converge."
Third, we will study her portrayals of Jansenistic grace in
"Parker's Back" and "The Comforts of Home." In our analysis of
these stories, we will show how O'Connor uses each of the three
literary devices we have previously described.

Thomistic Grace: "A Temple of the Holy Ghost"

Multivalent Symbols

In this brief story which recounts the sexual and spiritual
awakening and growth of a young girl of twelve, Flannery O'Connor
employs three multivalent symbols to present Thomistic grace.
The symbols are a hermaphrodite employed as a "freak" at the town
fair, the Host exposed in a monstrance at Benediction, and the
afternoon sun. These symbols represent male and female, human
and divine, and suffering and glory, respectively. These paired
meanings are juxtaposed to one another throughout the unfolding
story as opposites, that is, mutually exclusive meanings, in the
mind of the child.

The hermaphrodite displays both male and female physical
characteristics. The child wonders how one person can be both a
man and a woman at the same time without also having two heads.
The explanation by the "freak" that this condition is the will of
God does not significantly aid the child in understanding the
problem on the natural level, but provides a basis for the later
additional supernatural meaning of the symbol. "It" announces at
the beginning of the tent show:

> "God made me thisaway [sic] and if you laugh He may strike
> you the same way. This is the way He wanted me to be and
> I ain't disputing His way. I'm showing you because I got
> to make the best of it. I expect you to act like ladies
> and gentlemen. I never done it to myself nor had a thing
> to do with it but I'm making the best of it. I don't dis-
> pute hit [sic]" (p. 245).

The child is confused by these words and perceives this anomalous
occurrence as a riddle to be solved. She is eager to meditate
alone on its possible meaning. However, the naiveté of her sexual awareness is indicated when she tells her cousins the

fabricated story of having seen a rabbit give birth to six babies through its mouth.

The hermaphrodite's presence in the story introduces the "unexpected yet believable" aspect of grace which will be taken up again in each of the story's other symbols. It symbolizes the mystery of creation. What at first seems a freak on the natural level will become a manifestation of grace on the supernatural level. Male and female, natural and supernatural are then united harmoniously within the single symbol.

The second symbol is the Host which is exposed in a monstrance during the Benediction service the child attends when she and her mother return the visiting cousins to their convent school. The child, with an inadequate understanding of the meaning of the Eucharist, sees ivory-colored bread, but comes to realize more fully that it is also somehow Jesus. Trying to grasp this paradox of how the Host can be bread and God at the same time, the child's mind wanders back to the words of the freak: "I don't dispute hit [sic]. This is the way He wanted me to be" (p. 248). As in the case of the hermaphrodite who displays opposite concepts in a single unity, namely male and female physical characteristics in one body, so now there is presented a "Host" which is a single object, but contains within it two meanings. On the natural level it appears as ordinary bread, yet on the supernatural level its meaning is divine.

The third symbol is the afternoon sun. Just previous to her experience with the ivory Host at Benediction, the child notices the "ivory sun which was framed in the middle of the blue afternoon" (p. 247). This resplendent sun symbolizes the glory of creation and when related to the ivory Host signifies the glory of the resurrected Christ. As the child leaves the convent school chapel, having begun to realize the fuller meaning of the Eucharist, she sees the setting sun which appears "like an elevated Host drenched in blood," making a path in the sky "like a red clay road hanging over the trees" (p. 248). In this moment of vision, the sun comes to symbolize the suffering of the crucified Christ. Thus God and the human person, glory and suffering,

heaven and earth, and the supernatural and the natural become
harmonized into pregnant unities in the moment of grace.

As we have seen, O'Connor creates opposing meanings which
she later unites by a series of multivalent symbols. The added
supernatural meanings do not negate or destroy the natural allusions, but rather develop from them and bring them into harmony
and complementarity. The natural level is developed and enhanced by the disclosure of the supernatural meaning which,
though always present, is not seen until the moment of grace
which is its revelation. The twelve-year-old in this story finally experiences the gratuitous union of heaven and earth in the
joining of the setting sun with the red Georgia clay, the union
of male and female in the hermaphrodite at the fair, and the human and the divine in the Host at Benediction. These revelations
lead her to see that she too is both very ordinary and yet spiritually gifted. Her growth in understanding yields an unexpected,
ennobled view of reality, yet these opposite aspects contained
within each symbol have been present as integral elements throughout the development of the narrative. The opposition of the
meanings contained within the multivalent symbols is not destroyed or rejected in the moment of grace, but rather the separate meanings of both opposed elements are recognized and both
are united in dynamic tension within the complex symbols. The
revealed supernatural meanings ennoble and complete the natural
meanings. Hence, in this story grace builds on nature, an example of a Thomistic grace narrative.

Discrepancy in Action

In this story, the discrepancy in action between the intention and the outcome is one of degree, not direction. The story
itself is one of a confirmation. The child is beginning to move
toward adulthood. Throughout the story she ponders her future.
She notes the superficiality of her older cousins and the stupid-
ity and error of others. Her natural intention is to become a
person of importance. She fantasizes about becoming a war hero,
a doctor or an engineer. She realizes that to become a saint or

a martyr would be even more significant, but she disregards these possibilities due to her personal lack of virtue.

The additional notion that she may indeed have supernatural value is introduced through her cousins who refer to one another as "Temple One" and "Temple Two." She begins to identify with this concept: "I am a temple of the Holy Ghost, she said to herself and was pleased with the phrase. It made her feel as if somebody had given her a present" (p. 238). As she considers the term, the potential significance is only of intellectual interest. However, when she attends Benediction at the chapel of the girls' school, she begins to experience a subtle change in her own behavior. Her "ugly" thoughts cease. She first becomes quiet and empty-minded. Then, when the priest raises the monstrance, her mind is flooded with the image of the freak at the fair. Its works re-echo: "I don't dispute hit [sic]. This is the way He [God] wants me to be" (p. 248). The result of this thinking is a feeling of spiritual confirmation. If God creates and sustains the hermaphrodite, so surely does He confirm her life and its future. She feels ennobled and uplifted. Her growth direction has not been disrupted, but the maturing process entails something more than she had originally expected. She has undergone an experience of grace which takes the form of an understanding of her own natural growth process in relation to the spiritual value of her life. She has become "a person of importance," but not merely on the natural level she had originally imagined.

Moment of Recognition

In the moment of recognition, the twelve-year-old girl experiences an epiphany which confirms her new maturity. Whereas in the beginning of the story she thought of herself as an ugly child incapable of virtue, she now identifies herself as a "temple of the Holy Ghost" and comes to some understanding of the meaning of the concept.

At the beginning of the narrative, the child feels superior to her "stupid cousins" and holds her family's long-faced and nearly friendless boarder, Miss Kirby, in disdain. When the

cousins introduce the notions of themselves as "temples of the
Holy Ghost," the child identifies with the idea and feels ennobled. She feels as though someone has given her a gift. Here we
have the first interior movement which signifies the gentle action of grace uplifting nature. The remainder of the story presents the development of this early recognition.

The full recognition of the meaning of the phrase, "temple
of the Holy Ghost," comes at the conclusion of the narrative and
includes the further understanding of the three multivalent symbols and their relationship to one another in light of the central concept of person as "temple." These symbols, as we recall,
are the "freak," the Host at Benediction and the setting sun. As
the child is returning home, the taxi driver mentions that the
freak show has been closed down by the city officials. On hear-
ing the news, the child turns her eyes from the driver to the sun
setting over the highway. The brilliant red-ivory sun reminds
her of the Host at Benediction and of the hermaphrodite. Her
mind is illuminated through the juxtaposition of these two paradoxical symbols in the red-ivory light.

The child comes to realize that to be a human person in the
Christian sense of a "temple" consists of knowing and accepting
one's natural condition, as the freak does, and of being open to
the uplifting and ennobling power of the supernatural which is
manifest in the Host as the presence of God on earth. The red-
ivory color of the sunset reinforces the meaning of the symbols.
The red symbolizes the suffering of humankind (the rejection of
the freak and the crucifixion of Christ) and earthliness (the
sun makes a red path in the sky reflecting the person's path on
the red Georgia clay); the ivory symbolizes the glory of God (also present in the Benediction Host image) and the true, graced
state of humankind. The child's recognition thus comes through
the illuminating moment of the natural "benediction" at the end
of her journey. It confirms her supernatural value, while ac-
knowledging her natural limitations and physical personhood.

"A Temple of the Holy Ghost" explores a presentation of
grace analogous to Thomism. O'Connor has used the literary

devices in specific modes which portrays grace as uplifting and ennobling nature.[2]

Thomistic Grace: "The Artificial Nigger"

Multivalent Symbols

In this narrative, O'Connor employs one central symbol, an "artificial nigger." The symbol is complex and refers throughout the story not only (1) to a specific plaster statue of a black man eating a watermelon, but also (2) to the manner in which persons are reduced to "niggers" through human action, especially to the way in which white persons have related to Blacks in the South,[3] and (3) to the dark unknown and destructive forces in life. Utilizing the second connotation of the term, the popular expression for the white race's domination over and disdain

---

[2] In this story O'Connor also includes explicit "religious elements," many of which are direct references to Thomas Aquinas. The convent school which the cousins attend is "Mount St. Scholastica." During Benediction the hymn is the "Tantum Ergo," written by Thomas. The same hymn recurs elsewhere in the tale. There is a reference to a person as a "dumb ox." (Aquinas is often symbolized by hagiographers as "the dumb ox.") These external elements are secondary to our primary analysis of structural devices, but the allusions are striking and reinforce the literary mode.

[3] As we will observe in our discussion of O'Connor's use of the literary symbols in this story, the resolution of the "nigger" symbol has only minor social justice implications. O'Connor's primary interest is not in the application of Christian teaching to moral or ethical issues. We will see in the next chapter, for example, that social activists do not receive her approval. Rather, O'Connor's primary concern is the symbolic meaning which the oppressed Black suggests in her economy of graced salvation. She states in this regard: "It's fashionable to say that the South has a guilt complex on account of the Negro. The South has a sense of guilt and evil that is much more primal than any such relatively recent historical situation could account for. In Southern literature the Negro, without losing his identity, is a figure for our darker selves, our shadow side" (Unpublished manuscript, Flannery O'Connor Collection). This is similar to her approach to the Civil War, which she understands not as a wrong to be righted but as a lesson of human sinfulness and an opportunity for grace.

for the American Negro, as the initial literal meaning of the symbol, O'Connor creates a simple initiation narrative which depicts Thomistic grace.

The protagonist in the story is Mr. Head,[4] the grandfather of Nelson. Mr. Head sees himself as the boy's teacher and guide. He plans an excursion into the city in order to initiate the boy into the knowledge of good and evil. He divides the world into two parts: good, which he equates with whiteness, and evil, which he equates with blackness. Black people symbolize for him all that is evil, destructive and unknown. Earlier he had participated in forcing all the black people in his area to move out, thus in his mind purifying the countryside. He now plans an excursion into the city, which he claims is full of these black people, in order to initiate Nelson into the knowledge of good and evil. Though himself born in the city and only later brought to the country to live with his grandfather, Nelson has not seen a "nigger." Mr. Head claims that the boy will be unable to recognize one. Thus, as they start out from the all-white rural area where they live, Mr. Head sets as the boy's primary task the identification of a "nigger." The "nigger" symbolizes both the rejected Blacks and the evil unknown otherness in human life. This latter meaning is gradually developed through the pair's encounters with three "niggers" during their journey.

The first encounter with a "nigger" is with a mulatto man on the train. Mr. Head is pleased when Nelson fails to recognize the man as a Negro. When Mr. Head directs Nelson's attention to his ignorance in the matter, Nelson begins to experience his first hatred for "niggers." He has been humiliated and feels deceived that the man is not "black" but only "tan" in color. The existence of a person who is part white and part black has not occured to him as a possibility. He is thus initiated by Mr.

---

[4]His surname indicates not only his position of authority with regard to Nelson, but suggests as well his affinity to Adam, the "head" of the human race, who also sought the knowledge of good and evil.

Head into his society's discriminatory stance toward Blacks. This encounter also reveals that reality cannot always be separated easily into categories of black and white.

The second encounter, which occurs when they lose their way in the city, is with a black woman to whom Nelson feels sexually attracted and by whom he is maternally accepted. The juxtaposition of the awakening of sexual passion and yearning for his absent mother with the fact of the woman's blackness enables O'Connor to enrich the symbol beyond its initial meaning of hatred of "niggers" to include desire, hunger, fear, shame, and loss of personal control in relation to the dark unknown other. Mr. Head once again seizes the opportunity to point out Nelson's ignorance as shown in this second failure to identify and dominate the situation. Mr. Head compares Nelson's experience with the black woman to another unknown, the city's sewer system. He suggests that the devouring potential of the black woman is analogous to the endless underground sewerage system which is filled with refuse and rats. Overcome by the extent of his apparent ignorance and the terrible dangers of both the city and its "niggers," Nelson clings in total dependence to Mr. Head. Through this comparison, Mr. Head succeeded in reducing the child from his original naive pride at having himself been born in the city and his insistence on his own natural capabilities to recognize a "nigger" to a state of humiliation and insecurity. In short, Mr. Head has made Nelson his "nigger" by depriving the boy of human dignity and personal integrity.

The third encounter with a "nigger" takes place after Mr. Head abandons Nelson in the city. When the frightened child finally finds his grandfather and requires his help, he denies even knowing the boy. They walk on through the streets estranged from one another and alienated by the complexities of the city. At this point, the third "nigger" appears in the form of a plaster statue on a suburban lawn. Its appearance is totally unexpected by Mr. Head, who cannot believe it is a "nigger" because "niggers" are not important enough to have statues made of them. In fact, he believes that "niggers" are to be avoided, not

indicated and collected. Mr. Head has never seen a statue of
a black person before. Yet this "artificial nigger" become
the culmination of their quest.

> It was not possible to tell if the artificial Negro were
> meant to be young or old; he looked too miserable to be
> either. He was meant to look happy because his mouth was
> stretched up at the corners but the chipped eye and the
> angle he was cocked at gave him a wild look of misery in-
> stead (p. 268).

The statue itself is dilapidated, worn by the weather and in
ruins. Its appearance blurs normal distinctions. It will become
a unifying force in the resolution of the conflict. Within this
single symbol, all of the accumulated meaning of "nigger" is contained.

The "artificial nigger" is neither old nor young. In this
it is like Mr. Head and Nelson, whose age difference has been
obliterated by their exhausting and confusing experiences in the
city. Like them, too, the statue gives the appearance of misery
despite the original intention that it appear happy. Natural
circumstances have intervened to give the statue a "wild look."
In all of this, Nelson and his grandfather can easily identify
with the "nigger's" condition.

> They stood gazing at the artificial Negro as if they were
> faced with some great mystery, some monument to another
> victory that brought them together in their common defeat.
> They could feel it dissolving their differences like an
> action of mercy (p. 269).

The gratuitous appearance of the statue reunites the Heads.
In the face of this completely unexpected, but believable manifestation, they come to identify with the sufferings of the "nigger" and to understand how little they know of black people, life
in the city and themselves. Here the grandfather and the boy are
presented with a concrete reality which recapitulates their
frightening experiences in the city. It symbolizes their quest
in such a way as to suggest a *rapprochement* between the opposites
which had divided them. The "artificial nigger," which encompas-
ses the earlier meanings of the "nigger" symbol, effects a harmony between black and white, and between Mr. Head and Nelson.
In a paradoxical way this new "nigger" ennobles and enriches the

Heads.

Discrepancy in Action

In "The Artificial Nigger," then, Flannery O'Connor uses the multivalent symbol of the statue of the black man to expand and complete the meaning of the natural events in the narrative by an action of grace. In the same story, this concept of grace as enhancing and uplifting nature is also portrayed through the use of the literary device of discrepancy in action between intention and outcome.

The central action in the story involves Mr. Head's plan to initiate his grandson into a deeper understanding of the world through a guided tour of the city. Here they will directly encounter evil by examining the city and mingling with black people. Mr. Head expects that his grandson's successful education will be marked by three results: (1) the boy's ability to identify a "nigger," (2) his knowledge that the city is an evil place to which he should not return, and (3) his acknowledgement that his grandfather is a wise and able guide through life. In other words, he intends this journey to improve Nelson's ability to discriminate between "black and white," to demonstrate the existence of evil to the boy, and to prove his own superiority to the child.

Mr. Head himself begins the journey in moonlight, which O'Connor uses to symbolize his limited ability to make clear distinctions. Despite his belief that he understands life and is thus a "suitable guide for the young" (p. 195), he is gradually revealed to possess little actual knowledge of the city, of black people or of his own dark destructive side. His guided educational tour moves him from the safety and shadows of his rural moonlit clearing into the glaring sunlight of the city. His action, intended to teach Nelson a lesson, leads to a much deeper knowledge of reality for the old man himself.

In the first of the three encounters with Blacks, Mr. Head is shaken from his initial serenity and feeling of control over the situation. He notices the mulatto man on the train. The Negro

has appeared prematurely with regard to the plan because the pair
has not yet reached the city. In addition, the man is only part
black. Combinations of black and white have not been discussed
by Mr. Head. He had described the city as clearly divided into
"black and white." In preparing Nelson for the trip, he has explained that the boy may not like the city as "it'll be full of
niggers" (p. 197). Nelson has thought of "niggers" as completely
black and inhabiting only the city. Thus, when he encounters the
mulatto on the train, he fails to recognize him as a "nigger."
Mr. Head not only recognizes the man immediately, but in the wake
of his vexation at seeing a Negro who is not totally black and
who is on the train instead of in the city, his confident verbose
manner is suddenly replaced by silence and a fierce, cautious
look comes into his eyes. Nelson sees only "a man" (p. 200), "a
fat man," "an old man." Mr. Head tells him that the man is a
"nigger" and comments that Nelson is ignorant because he has
failed to recognize him.

The first victory for Mr. Head is quickly forgotten as the
tour of the city proper begins. Nelson realizes that the old man
has lost his sense of direction as they wander the streets in a
circle. In addition, he remarks that Mr. Head has forgotten their
food on the train. Thus when they begin to get hungry from
walking, they have no provisions for lunch. Through these two
minor events, Mr. Head begins to notice that he is not as totally
in control as he had intended to be. Nelson asserts that they
are lost because of Mr. Head's ignorance. He suggests that they
ask directions from one of the Blacks who inhabit this section of
the city. Mr. Head gives the responsibility back to Nelson,
since Nelson lays claim to having been born in the city and has
recognized the fact that they are lost. Nelson, thinking himself too afraid to ask a Negro man or child, seeks out a black
woman standing in the doorway of her home. Nelson is drawn by
the woman's dark eyes and her cool response. He becomes sexually
attracted to the woman. The experience both excites and frightens him. It is his first sexual encounter. The woman encompas-
ses motherhood, sexual pleasure and the dark stranger. He is on

the verge of collapse when his grandfather intervenes to snatch him away. Feeling his own shame and his grandfather's anger, the boy meekly takes the old man's hand as a sign of his dependence. At this point, Mr. Head believes that he is finally beginning to achieve his goal, which is to teach the boy the danger of the city as symbolized in the Negro. Mr. Head begins to take pride in his achievement and to press Nelson for an admission of his superiority and the boy's ignorance.

In light of the boy's reluctance to admit complete defeat, Mr. Head begins to design a final aspect of his action to confirm the boy's knowledge of evil and his dependence on his grandfather. He proposes that they rest from their journey, and once Nelson is asleep Mr. Head hides from the boy's view. His intention is to produce in him the terror of abandonment in the city and to make him realize his need of his grandfather. To wake the boy, he bangs on the garbage can behind which he is hiding. Startled by the commotion, Nelson awakes. Realizing that his grandfather is not in sight, he dashes down the street, accidentally knocking over an elderly woman. When passers-by accuse the boy, the grandfather is noticed, but denies knowing him or having responsibility for the event. Thus he completely severs the relationship in order to reinforce the boy's utter alienation in the city without his guide and protector.

Finally the grandfather quits the scene and is followed at a distance by the angry Nelson. Gradually the grandfather realizes that he has over-extended the lesson and lost the boy's respect and affection. The result is that Nelson has gained a new dignity and the grandfather requires, for the first time in his memory, the boy's forgiveness. The grandfather has revealed his own *dark* side. To compensate for his error, Mr. Head offers to buy the boy a cold drink, but his offer is ignored. He then discovers a water spigot. He feels unworthy, but stoops to take a drink and offers one to Nelson, who refuses the shared water. Mr. Head realizes now the intensity of the anger the boy holds for him. Nelson seems bent on preserving the worst of the old man's treatment of him, and focuses on his anger at the old man's betrayal,

a manifestation of Mr. Head's dark or evil aspect. As the grandfather despairs of ever being reconciled to the boy, they come to
a statue of a black figure.

　　Like the water spigot, the statue is completely unexpected,
yet it is quite believable in the white suburbs into which they
have by now strayed. However, unlike the water, this phenomenon
is compelling to both of them. They have spent the entire trip
considering the recognition of the Negro. Now they are confronted with one which seems to them to convey a mystery beyond their
ability to grasp. It is plaster, not real. Someone has made a
Negro. In their minds, Negroes have signified evil which can be
detected and avoided. Further, it recombines the qualities Mr.
Head has sought to divide. It is both old and young, white and
black, in time and out of time. Its presence compounds their
petty differences by confronting them with a mystery which they
can experience, but cannot verbalize. It is witness to some
knowledge larger than themselves, a testimony to the unity of
black and white and the relationship between good and evil.

　　The statue becomes the instrument of their reconciliation.
It restores dignity to Mr. Head's action on the natural level.
This "nigger" is indeed difficult to recognize, yet Nelson is
able to identify it immediately. Their mutual recognition of
the statue and astonishment at its existence heals the rift between them. Neither has adequate words to explain why anyone
would manufacture a "nigger" and place it as a decoration on the
lawn. In the face of this total surprise, even to the "wise" Mr.
Head, they are able to acknowledge their ignorance of the ways
of the city and to renew their need for dependence upon one another. Their relationship is now renewed on a deeper level.

　　In addition to the restoration of his friendship with Nelson,
a natural healing, Mr. Head also experiences the forgiveness of
his sin, a spiritual healing. Whereas he experienced "hell" not
only in his denial of Nelson and Nelson's rejection of him, but
also in his personal failure as a teacher, he now understands
that the statue's gratuitous appearance both represents his own
dark side and frees him from it. He feels the forgiveness of his

sinful pride and the accompanying comfort of divine mercy. This revelation of his own true nature and his need for forgiveness is in addition to Mr. Head's original intention. However, it does not replace or reverse the natural intent, but rather extends and develops his goal: the quest of knowledge.

Nelson has, in fact, accomplished the three tasks set by Mr. Head as the purpose of their journey. He has learned to identify a "nigger"; he has experienced the danger of the city; and he does now admit his grandfather's wisdom in such matters. As they disembark from the train that has finally returned them to their rural home, Nelson tells his grandfather: "I'm glad I've went once, but I'll never go back again!" (p. 270).

Mr. Head's and Nelson's experiences on this journey are intended by O'Connor to reflect the in-breaking of the supernatural into the natural course of action in such a way as to depict grace as ennobling their natural acts. In this Thomistic story, the discrepancy between the protagonist's original intention and the outcome of his action results from the revelation of another (Divine) intention which completes the natural (human) intention and adds to it an elevating supernatural outcome. The action is thus brought forward by the intervention of grace. The original direction of the protagonist is furthered by a grace which is continuous with it.

Moment of Recognition

We have examined O'Connor's use of symbol and discrepancy in action. Her use of the third device, the moment of recognition, is intimately related to these two techniques. In our examination of the multivalent symbol, the "artificial nigger," we observed that the symbol's meaning is expanded to encompass the Heads' experiences, both real and projected, before and during their trip. As O'Connor develops the symbol, it takes on more varied significance. Finally its meaning culminates in a *rapprochement* between sets of opposite meanings, thus indicating through symbolism the nature-unifying aspect of Thomistic grace. Likewise, in the heart of the grace-event, Mr. Head's original

intentions are accomplished, but an added divine intention ennobles and enriches the experience indicating the relative poverty
of his natural (ungraced) intention. The supernatural plan uplifts Mr. Head and reunites him with his estranged grandson.

The reunification and enrichment found in the grace-event
as presented in "The Artificial Nigger" are accomplished in the
moment of recognition. Because it is essentially Mr. Head whose
nature is uplifted and his plan which is complemented by something better and more meaningful, it is he who most fully participates in this awareness.

The preparation for the moment of recognition begins in "The
Artificial Nigger" immediately after a singularly significant action: Mr. Head's denial of Nelson. Through this evil act Mr.
Head had intended to confirm Nelson's ultimate dependence on his
grandfather. His intention does not bear the fruit he expected.
Instead of Nelson's gratitude and dependence, Mr. Head's action
has generated the boy's uncontrolled hatred and has revealed both
to himself and to Nelson his own dark, destructive side. Mr.
Head begins to realize the result of his action and to feel
guilty for the first time in his life. He tries some conciliato-
ry moves toward Nelson. Each is rejected. Mr. Head's alienation
grows. He loses hope that he will be able to make peace with the
boy. He begins to entertain other desperate, destructive ideas.
He ponders dropping himself into a dark sewer which would carry
him silently into the bowels of the city (an anticipation of his
later identification with the "nigger"). He does not believe
that Nelson would be concerned at his loss. He feels like someone
shipwrecked on an abandoned island. Finally he calls out, "Oh
Gawd [sic] I'm lost!" (p. 211).

Mr. Head means his desperate cry to be understood on the
literal level. Yet the introduction of the word "Gawd" and the
building references to the *hell* of alienation, the complete loss
of human hope for *salvation*, and his awareness of Nelson's *judgment* all point beyond their secular connotations toward the religious level of meaning which O'Connor will highlight in the moment of recognition. As Mr. Head's agony grows, he begins to

think of himself as a sinner and to judge himself guilty as he imagines God might judge him. Thus, his first recognition is that of his moral and spiritual guilt. He is himself a spiritual "nigger." In himself he recognizes the depravity of the one left to his own devices and unaided by grace. From the depths of despair, Mr. Head is gratuitously saved through the unexpected manifestation of the artificial nigger.

The statue of the nigger heals and uplifts Mr. Head's self-image. Not through any act or merit of his own, but in a purely unanticipated and unexpected way, the statue appears. As we noted above, O'Connor has carefully prepared throughout the story for its appearance, and its symbolic value is such that it is able to draw together the opposites identified in the development of the whole tale. In the symbol, the differences between Mr. Head and Nelson, between the white and the black, between the young and the old, between the utilitarian and the useless, between good and evil, are all encompassed in a universal symbol of human suffering. In confrontation with the statue and the value it bears, Mr. Head moves to the second moment of recognition. Here his first insight regarding his depravity is not reversed or eliminated, but conjoined to it is the recognition that he is also forgiven and loved. Thus he comes to the perception that he has received the totally free and undeserved gift of God's mercy. This mercy accepts Mr. Head in his fallen state and uplifts him. He feels restored and enhanced through the experience.

Mr. Head thus comes to recognize, in a moment of greater spiritual understanding, the uniting power of grace. He has seen his natural intention moved beyond its own potential. He and Nelson are united as never before in the reconciling union made possible by the active presence of God's grace. Such a use of the moment of recognition to complete and enhance nature characterizes O'Connor's Thomistic portrayals of grace. Mr. Head, after the grace-event, continues his natural existence and his relationship to Nelson. They return to their rural home. There has been no radical reversal of their natural lives to disrupt this relationship (the kind of disruption which, as we shall see,

typifies O'Connor's Augustinian and Jansenistic stories). Yet
Mr. Head has been changed. His new state is both a continuation
of his original natural condition and a change to a fuller life.
He recognizes this growth, and his recognition is a spiritual
maturation based on a greater understanding of the uniting and
ennobling mercy of God's grace.

* * *

We have now completed our study of two Thomistic stories: "A
Temple of the Holy Ghost" and "The Artificial Nigger." In both
Flannery O'Connor uses literary devices in specific ways, depicting an operation of grace which acts in relative harmony with nature, continuing and perfecting its purpose, elevating it to a
new dimension of spiritual maturity.

In the next section of this chapter, we will turn to a study
of two Augustinian stories. Here we will note a striking change
in approach. The operation of grace will be more apparent, since
grace will serve to oppose and reverse the workings of sinful nature. In the Thomistic stories we have just examined, grace is
present, but its action is less startling since it works harmoniously, often almost without notice, along with the natural level
of the story.

It is interesting to note in this context that "The Artificial Nigger" requires a special kind of ending. In comparison to
the Augustinian stories, the action of grace develops gradually
and "naturally" in "The Artificial Nigger." Hence, it might seem
to occur through a happy accident (the discovery of the statue)
or through human good will. Perhaps it is for this reason that
O'Connor does something which she never does in an Augustinian
story. She moralizes at the end of the tale to indicate her own
intention with regard to the meaning of the grace-event. She
tells the reader that the story's resolution is a direct result
of God's action. The author intervenes in this way presumably
because Thomistic grace, working through human nature, might not
be construed by the reader as divine intervention. She must tell
the reader that the apparently "natural" or "fortuitous" development

is in fact a divine intervention working in a natural way.

Augustinian Grace: "Greenleaf"

Quite different from the depictions of grace we have described in "A Temple of the Holy Ghost" and "The Artificial Nigger" are O'Connor's portrayals of the operations of grace in her Augustinian stories. "Greenleaf" is an example.

Multivalent Symbols

"Greenleaf" recounts the attempt of a widowed mother of two sons to maintain a successful dairy business in order to provide a secure economic and social future for herself and her family. The central symbol in the story is a "scrub bull" who has strayed onto the farm threatening the purity of the herd strain and the breeding schedule. On the natural level the bull is seen by Mrs. May in its unrestrained and impure sexuality as a threat to her economic security. On the supernatural level the bull symbolizes the force of divine love. The action of grace rejects the natural meaning of the symbol and affirms the supernatural one.

Mrs. May, the farm owner, views the stray bull as a natural destructive force which, if not restrained, will impregnate her cows, reducing the quality of her stock, and ultimately bring about her financial ruin. The bull also symbolizes for her the inferior (scrub) persons with whom she finds herself surrounded, the Greenleafs. They are the tenant family who work on her farm. Mr. Greenleaf is unambitious and shiftless; Mrs. Greenleaf is a "prayer healer" and a poor housekeeper; the two Greenleaf sons have married well, have numerous children, own their own home and run a competive dairy farm in the area. All of this irritates Mrs. May, who has judged the Greenleafs and found them lacking; yet life seems to treat this undeserving and unvirtuous family generously.

Mrs. May complains that she must struggle just to "get by." Her farm has not been modernized because she cannot afford the expense entailed; her help is dawdling and indifferent; her own

sons are both unmarried and unproductive; and she alone is concerned to provide for their future. Unlike Mr. Greenleaf, who is
lazy and disinterested in his work, she is industrious. Unlike
Mrs. Greenleaf, who is an unkempt religious fanatic, she seeks to
maintain order and subscribes to the principle that all things
should be taken in moderation. She is a liberal Christian who
neither believes the truths of her religion nor allows it to
"warp" her. She considers herself to be justified by the way she
conducts her life. When called before the seat of judgment, she
will be able to say: "I've worked, I have not wallowed" (p. 332).
She will be able to substantiate this statement in relation to
her judgment of both Mr. and Mrs. Greenleaf.

In addition to the natural significance of the bull as an
insatiable, inferior beast who symbolizes for Mrs. May on the one
hand the natural destruction of her dairy farm and on the other
the Greenleaf family, O'Connor suggests from the outset of the
story a supernatural significance in the bull's appearance on
Mrs. May's farm. He is described initially as "some patient god
come down to woo [Mrs. May]" (p. 311). This "uncouth country
suitor" comes from the east, wearing a piece of hedge like a
"prickly crown" (p. 312). The "god" who comes down (to earth) as
a suitor or lover, wearing a crown (of thorns) clearly suggests
that the bull is a symbol of Christ on the supernatural level.

This Christ imagery, which O'Connor will use most clearly at
the moment of recognition at the end of the story, is also inter-
jected into the narrative by Mrs. Greenleaf, the "scrub" tenant
woman who in her "inferior" social origin and style of life and
sexuality (she has numerous children) resembles the bull. During
her prayer healing exercises, she rolls in the dirt, crying out,
"Jesus." "The sound was so piercing that she [Mrs. May] felt as
if some violent unleashed force had broken out of the ground and
was charging toward her." (p. 316). Even the name Jesus does violence to this liberal believer. It too, like the bull, seems to
be charging to devour her. She regards the name as a private ut-
terance, not to be said in public, like words referring to sex.
When Mrs. Greenleaf's prayer continues with anguish and emotion to

its conclusion: "Jesus, stab me in the heart!" (p.317), Mrs. May is angry and disgusted. She considers it obscene to wallow in the dirt and call out to God. Unable to think that Jesus could condone such action, she chastizes Mrs. Greenleaf, telling her that Jesus "would tell you to get up from there this instant and go wash your children's clothes" (p. 317). Though Mrs. May is indifferent to religion, she suggests that to be purely religious means to live a life of physical and emotional restraint, cleanliness and respectability.

In the final moment of grace, the words of Mrs. Greenleaf's prayer are enacted by the bull. He attacks Mrs. May, burying "his head in her lap, like a wild tormented lover. One of his horns sank until it pierced her heart and the other curved around her side and held her in an unbreakable grip" (p.333). The bull has become the supernatural lover. Mrs. May's understanding of the bull as a natural symbol for the destruction of her dairy is reversed. The bull's true meaning is revealed to exist on the supernatural level. While he destroys her natural life, he points to a supernatural love which both reverses human values and brings a call to conversion. We will return to the question of Mrs. May's conversion when we discuss the moment of recognition.

Another symbol, which is less obvious, but which operates in a similar way in the story, is that of the farm itself. Mrs. May views the farm as her ecomonic "salvation." She states: "I am a poor woman and this place is all I have. I have two boys to educate" (p. 316). She jealously guards her land and her pure strain of dairy cows in order to make a profit. In contrast, Mrs. Greenleaf holds the land, and life in general, to be sacred. While Mrs. May struggles to control her environment, to protect it against the destructive forces (the bull and the inferior Greenleafs) that would defeat her economically, Mrs. Greenleaf, a religious kind of earth mother, gathers all the problems and tragedies of the world (in the form of newspaper clippings) and buries them in the earth, conducting a prayer-healing service over them. She begs Jesus to pour forth his mercy on humankind. Thus through Mrs. Greenleaf, the "inferior" white trash woman, the spiritual meaning of the land is presented.

In the moment of grace, when the sacred bull emerges from
the earth to devour her, Mrs. May's understanding of the farm is
reversed: "the tree line was a dark wound in a world that was
nothing but sky" (p. 333). Her farm thus seems to Mrs. May no
longer a source of profit, but a sacred source of redemptive
grace, a wound which brings salvation. Thus the meaning of the
land as understood by Mrs. May on the (sinful) natural level is
opposed by a supernatural meaning which is shown to be the only
meaning acceptable to God's will. The natural meaning of the
land as understood by Mrs. May, like that of the bull, is rejected in favor of a supernatural meaning, which alone is affirmed by
the action of grace.

Discrepancy in Action

The human protagonist in "Greenleaf" is Mrs. May, who intends to live a long and productive life through the operation of
a profitable dairy business. An intrusion into the course of her
daily affairs, namely the appearance in her pasture of a scrub
bull, causes her to take a specific course of action. To preserve her herd's quality and the milk production schedule, she
must rid the farm of the unwanted, inferior bull.

Her initial plan is merely to have her farm hand, Mr. Greenleaf, drive the animal from her property. When this fails and
the animal returns to her pasturelands, she decides that the bull
must be destroyed. By the time of the invention of this second
plan, two developments have occured which heighten the significance of the intended action: (1) Mrs. May has discovered that
the bull actually belongs to the Greenleaf sons, and (2) the bull
has been tearing up the hedge under Mrs. May's bedroom window.
The discovery of the bull's ownership explains to Mrs. May the
reason that Mr. Greenleaf has not made a serious effort to drive
the bull away. It is feeding largely on her property. This increases her anger at the Greenleafs, whom she believes to be
prospering at her expense. She sees her decision to force Mr.
Greenleaf to shoot the bull as a way to regain her authority over

the pastureland and to assert her power over her farm hand. The presence during the night of the devouring (sexually active) bull under her bedroom window has also frightened Mrs. May. She identifies him as an unspecified force which has been gradually eroding her property and which now seems also to threaten her personal well-being. She now has an emotional investment as well as economic concern in the death of the bull.

To insure that the bull is killed and to gain the personal satisfaction of presiding over the event, Mrs. May decides to drive Mr. Greenleaf into the pasture after the bull. As they drive into the field, the bull is contentedly eating amid the herd. Mr. Greenleaf gets out of the car intending to force the bull into a smaller unused pasture. Finally, after several unsuccessful attempts, Mr. Greenleaf strikes the bull with a sharp rock which he has hurled at him. The bull gallops into a surrounding woods. Mr. Greenleaf follows slowly after him. Mrs. May waits at the car.

After some time, when neither the farm hand nor the bull have emerged from the woods, Mrs. May sounds the car's horn and returns to her expectant position on the car's bumper. The bull emerges from the woods, coming toward her at a slow gallop. While she calls the bull's location to Mr. Greenleaf, the bull moves steadily toward her and gores her with his horns. She remains frozen in unbelief as she realizes the intent of the bull's action and experiences the result.

Mrs. May had intended to assure her economic security, to demonstrate her control over the affairs of her dairy farm, and to preserve her personal well-being by destroying the Greenleaf's bull. However, her action is interrupted and her intention reversed. Instead of her presiding over the killing of the animal, the bull attacks her. Through the action of the bull, Mrs. May is brought to a moment of conversion. She is forced to see that she is not ultimately in control of her destiny, and that in wrongly valuing her material goods and warding off the divine lover, she has chosen a merely natural goal which grace must ultimately reverse. Her plan to provide for her economic security

not only fails, but is revealed to be sinful. In the face of a
divine intention which upholds a supernatural value, her own intention is both petty and futile. The bull's intrusion has been
an action of grace through which the natural intention is reversed and the divine intention revealed.

Moment of Recognition

The recognition in "Greenleaf" occurs at the moment when
Mrs. May's intention is effectively reversed by an intervening
divine will. At this same time, the plural meaning of the key
symbols is reinterpreted. One meaning is affirmed while another
is rejected. The protagonist is brought to a moment of conversion based on the reversal of her action and the revelation of
the true meaning, on the supernatural level, of the multivalent
symbols. Thus Mrs. May is forced to see the existence of another
order of values, one which invalidates her own quest for material
power and economic security and her false notions of human domination and natural providence. She is confronted with a spiritual order which opposes her. Through the reversal of her own
plan and the imposition of a divine will, she is confronted with
the reality of her human weakness in the face of supernatural
power. Her former understanding of reality is opposite to what
she now sees.

In the moment of recognition, Mrs. May stands firm. She is
powerless to escape her death. As the bull's horn pierces her
heart, "she continued to stare straight ahead but the entire
scene in front of her had changed--the tree line was a dark
wound in a world that was nothing but sky--and she had the look
of a person whose sight has been restored but who finds the light
unbearable" (p. 333). This supernatural vision is in radical opposition of her earlier sense of her own meaning and actions.
The shock of the revelation is overpowering. The grace consists
in the revelation of a divine intervention which opposes the order of natural will and intention. The reader is able only to
see the final shocked condition of Mrs. May in the death which
expresses this sovereignty of God.

O'Connor ends the tale with Mr. Greenleaf's interpretation of the final scene. He views Mrs. May as bent over the bull "whispering some last discovery into the animal's ear" (p. 334). For our purposes, Mrs. May's acceptance or rejection of this discovery is inconsequential to the earlier moment of recognition. The grace-event here culminates in the protagonist's awareness of her call to conversion or metanoia. Whether or not she is able to follow this call is not our concern.

"Greenleaf" is thus an Augustinian story. In its emphasis on opposition of symbolic meanings, on reversal of the protagonist's original intention, and on a recognized call to conversion, "Greenleaf" depicts an approach to grace which suggests analogy to Augustinianism. Grace opposes sinful nature.

Augustinian Grace: "Everything That Rises Must Converge"

Multivalent Symbols

The central multivalent symbol in "Everything That Rises Must Converge" is a new purple and green hat. Julian's mother,[5] one of the two central characters, ponders whether she is justified in having paid a substantial sum for the hat, which she intends to wear when she has to take public transportation downtown to her health class. To her mind, the purple and green hat makes her look distinguished. She tells her skeptical son, Julian, that "you only live once and paying a little more for it, I at least won't meet myself coming and going" (p. 406). For her, the purple and green hat symbolizes her true position in society and

---

[5]The actual name of the woman is in doubt. In the course of the story, the names "Chestny" and "Godhigh" are mentioned as family names, but the woman is never actually identified as having either surname, and it is indeed more likely that neither name is that of her dead husband. The only clear identification is that she is "Julian's mother." Critics have generally referred to her as "Mrs. Chestny," but recent scholoarship has pointed out the inadequacy of this choice (Hopkins, "Julian's Mother"). Hence we will use the accurate, if awkward "Julian's mother."

sets her apart from common women. She further reminds Julian
that he comes from a line of Southern landowners and political
leaders, the Chestnys, and that his grandmother was a "Godhigh."

Julian, the other main character, thinks that the hat looks
like a cushion which has lost its filling. To him, a college-
educated liberal, it symbolizes his mother's futile attempt to
live in the glory of the past and her inability to adapt to her
present socially and economically reduced situation amid the
changing mores of the South. He thinks the hat to be a hideous
symbol of her naive and prejudiced outlook on life.

Both of these meanings of the symbol pertain to the natural
level of the narrative. But O'Connor introduces another meaning
through her description early in the story. She describes the
hat's green and purple color as similar to a bruise, pointing
beyond the natural level to another meaning which will be revealed only at the climax of the story. At that moment, Julian's
and his mother's understandings of the hat's significance will be
reversed in the light of a supernatural meaning.

In donning the hat for her bus trip to the health class,
Julian's mother seeks to confirm her socially prominent past and
to assert her importance even in this racially mixed and socio-
economically unstable society. "With the world in the mess it's
in, it's a wonder you can go anywhere. Most of them in it are
not our kind of people, but I can be gracious to anybody. I know
who I am" (p. 407). According to her interpretation, the "mess"
in the world is caused by the changes in race relations and the
gradual decay of the old order. Despite the problems, however,
she knows her own position and the social manner and grace appropriate to her class. The hat symbolizes both her dignity and her
personal attempt to maintain the past order.

Julian replies that people "don't give a damn for your graciousness. Knowing who you are is good for one generation only.
You haven't the foggiest idea where you stand now or who you are"
(p. 407). Julian argues for a more tolerant and liberal understanding of the Black-White problem. Interpreting the hat as a
banner of her imaginary dignity, he holds in contempt his mother's

ethical thinking and her insistence on maintaining the old, discriminatory manners. His liberal attitude toward Blacks, though
eventually revealed to be superficial and unacceptable when
judged against a higher standard, seems initially to provide a
more enlightened perspective.

On the natural level, Julian sees the hat as a symbol of all
those people who, like his mother, are part of the problem. He
believes that the hat is perfectly appropriate for her thinking,
but he rejects such thinking. When a black woman wearing an
identical purple and green hat boards the bus, the symbolism of
the hat takes on more complexity. Julian first recognizes the
woman as his mother's black double. The hat now assumes in his
eyes a suggestion of "liberal" unity. He is delighted to realize
that his own attitude will be vindicated when his mother perceives that a black woman wears the exact type of hat that she
has chosen to set herself apart. His mother, however, fails to
recognize this meaning of the symbol.

Through a sequence of events, including especially her own
attempt to be gracious to the black woman's child, Julian's mother is forced into a violent confrontation with the black woman.
Here the additional meaning of the symbol is revealed. The hat
neither symbolizes uniqueness and elevated social stature as Julian's mother would have it, nor does it substantiate Julian's
liberal interpretation of racial equality. O'Connor does not accept either of these meanings. Rather, she proceeds beyond the
natural level to a supernatural significance. The hat comes to
reflect the bruised condition of all of humankind in relation to
its true dignity. Julian's mother's pride and self-esteem are
reversed. The black woman rejects her condescending action to
the child, and in her anger knocks her to the ground. Julian's
mother's whole notion of the world is here shown to be incorrect.
In the order of grace, all things are reversed. Her hat is
knocked off her head. She is humbled and her pride is dashed to
the ground. Worse yet, she now suffers a stroke and dies--the
result of the violent collision of her world view with the supernatural reality indicated by the appearance of her black double

who wears the identical purple and green hat.

Julian first believes that his insight is correct and that
his mother will now surely learn her lesson. The lesson, he believes, is that all persons are equal. What he fails to understand is the added dimension that all persons are equally guilty.
In the moment of grace, his social liberalism is reversed. His
mother has not learned; she has been killed as a result of her
effort to be kind--though condescending. In the divine order,
liberalism is irrelevant. Julian's mother loses not only her erroneous ideas, but her life. Julian loses his mother. He is
left at her death stripped of his arrogance and of his mother's
protection.

Thus the multivalent symbol, which from the beginning of the
story bore two natural meanings, one suggested by Julian's mother
and the other by Julian, has undergone a reversal. For different
reasons both Julian's and his mother's meanings have been rejected. In opposition to them is revealed the supernatural meaning.

Discrepancy in Action

The second literary technique, discrepancy in action between
intention and outcome, is used in "Everything That Rises Must
Converge" in such a way as to present the reversal of natural human intentions in the face of a divine or supernatural intention.
This device is used in conjunction with the actions of both Julian and his mother. The mother intends to be gracious to every-
one, even to those racially and socially inferior to her. Julian
intends to teach his mother the lesson that her type of graciousness to Blacks is unacceptable and embarrasses him in public. In
the moment of grace, the original intentions of both Julian and
his mother are reversed.

As the story begins, Julian's mother is preparing to go to
her weight-reducing class downtown. Her doctor has said that she
must lose twenty pounds in order to reduce her blood pressure and
improve her general state of health. However, she is unwilling
to ride the recently integrated public bus in the evenings alone.

Reminding Julian of all she has done for him, she insists that it is his duty to accompany her on the bus. He believes that she is being childish, creating an imaginary danger and requiring his "protection" for no reason. His attitude is that of a reluctant martyr for an unworthy cause.

During the bus ride, both Julian and his mother display openly their attitudes to the changing social situation. When they board the momentarily all-white bus, Julian is noticeably disappointed, but his mother happily remarks out loud that they have the bus "to themselves." She quickly gains support for this discriminatory position from the other white riders. Julian is outraged.

When Blacks begin to board the bus, Julian changes his seat in order to sit beside one as a silent protest of his mother's statement. This offends his mother. "From this position, he looked serenely across at his mother. Her face had turned angry red. He stared at her, making his eyes the eyes of a stranger. He felt his tension suddenly lift as if he had openly declared war on her" (p. 412). Though he is himself completely unsuccessful in engaging Blacks in conversation, Julian feels free of prejudice and able to handle the facts of the changing social order. From this "liberated" vantage point, he is able to cut himself off emotionally from his mother and to judge her objectively as small-minded, as a child.

He begins to ponder ways to teach her a lesson which will force her to act like an adult and make the best of the inevitable situation of integration. He considers refusing to leave the bus at their stop, making her walk the four blocks to the gymnasium alone. However, before he settles on a plan, his need is satisfied by the arrival on the bus of a black mother with a young son. The woman is his mother's black double. She wears a green and purple hat identical to hers and comports herself with a disdain for Whites equal to his mother's disdain for Blacks. Julian is delighted that "fate" has provided the opportunity for his mother's instruction. However, when his mother notices that the black woman wears a matching hat to hers, she is merely

amused. A look comes over her face "as if the woman were a mon-
key that had stolen her hat" (p. 416).

Julian's mother turns her attention from the black woman to
her four-year-old son. She remarks that the child is "cute."
The little boy is eager for attention and rushes from his mother's grasp toward Julian's mother. The black mother angrily
snatches him back, shouting for him to behave. Julian's mother
continues to attract the child's attention and as all four of
them rise to disembark at the same stop, Julian's mother begins
to reach into her purse to give the responsive child a nickel.
The gesture, quite automatic for his mother, sends Julian into
a frenzy. He tries to prevent what must only be interpreted by
the black mother as an act of condescension. However, his mother
succeeds in finding a shiny coin and presenting it to the child.
The black mother responds in rage shouting: "He don't take no-
body's pennies!" (p. 418). She knocks Julian's mother to the
pavement and, dragging her child, hurries down the street.

Julian tries to use the situation to his own advantage. He
remarks that she has deserved the treatment she has received. He
proclaims that the whole black race will no longer accept her
condescending pennies, that her old Southern manners are obsolete
and her graciousness offensive. "You needn't act as if the world
has come to an end because it hasn't. From now on you've got to
live in a new world and face a few realities for a change. Buck
up, it won't kill you" (p. 419).

Julian's words are ironic. The new world that his mother
faces is not the natural world of the changing South, but a supernatural world. The black woman's action has indeed killed his
mother. She suffers from a stroke and dies. Julian, who sought
merely to teach his mother a lesson in social justice, experiences the reversal of his intention. In this moment of grace, he
encounters the end of life as he has known it, characterized by
his dependency on his mother. In this, her last moment, he cries
out for help. She is swept away from him by a "tide of darkness." This same tide of darkness "seemed to sweep him back to
her, postponing from moment to moment his entry into the world of

guilt and sorrow" (p. 420). Julian's liberal racial attitudes and unsympathetic treatment of his mother are natural attitudes which are revealed to be inappropriate and inadequate in light of the supernatural order of values.

His mother, too, undergoes the reversal of her intention in the action of grace. What she had meant to be a gesture demonstrating her amiability and generosity has been judged to demean the black child. The action which she thought would raise her position in the eyes of the black woman and demonstrate for Julian proper behavior for one in their social position has in fact caused her social and physical downfall.

The journey which she had undertaken to enhance her physical health and reduce her weight and blood pressure produces the opposite result. Her blood pressure rises and she suffers a stroke. She has been not only physically and emotionally reduced, but she is brought to the moment of death. The shock of the violent reaction to her gesture and its outcome have turned her world upside down.

From the point of view of the supernatural order, her intention and her motivating understanding of reality have been opposed by a larger intention and a more powerful will. Her original intention to ensure physical well-being and to display generosity have been turned back on her by the action of grace. The black woman, acting as the instrument of grace, opposes her plans. The action of the black woman has introduced the existence of another order and a divine will whose meaning is far more pervasive and in radical opposition to the original goals which Julian's mother intended. This action of grace forces her to the limits of her natural existence and its self-created manner and values. She is forced to realize the existence of something larger than herself, which reveals a supernatural intention and judges her acts not with regard to her petty self-centered intention, but in relation to a larger, supernatural meaning. Here we note that the operation of grace has reversed both Julian's and his mother's original intentions. Thus, we have discrepancy used to depict Augustinian grace.

Moment of Recognition

In "Everything That Rises Must Converge," we have seen that
the meaning of the symbols and the intentions of human actions
undergo reversals in the moment of grace. So too, in this story,
the recognition is that of a reversal or call to conversion. In
having his mother suddenly wrenched from his life, Julian must
abandon his own childish ways and enter the adult world. His
mother's position is more extreme. She is forced to accept the
permanent loss of her past, her son and even her life. Her world
has been rejected and now, in death, she faces a total reversal
of her values in light of a supernatural order which ultimately
rules the universe.

Julian, who has seen himself to be more liberal and "broad-
minded" than his mother, able to handle the fact of the changing
racial patterns in the new South in a way his immature and un-
enlightened mother cannot, comes in the moment of grace to recognize that he, too, has only a naive understanding of the complexities of the racial problem and that he has rejected the woman on
whom he has been completely dependent. In having declared "war"
on his mother for a cause he barely understands and cannot himself adequately handle, he has lost her completely. With his
mother's death, his childhood comes to an abrupt halt. Though
he calls out, "Mama," to her in her last few moments, they are
like strangers. He looks at "a face he had never seen before"
(p. 420). Her face is completely distorted by the pain involved
in the total experience. Her one eye is fixed, staring at something in the distance. Her other eye "remained fixed on him,
raked his face again, found nothing and closed" (p. 420). He
recognizes their complete alienation from one another and is now
called to acknowledge his guilt on this account and to repent.
Through the action of grace, he is brought to experience the
"world of guilt and sorrow" symbolized in the supernatural order
by his mother's bruise-colored hat.

His mother recognizes the reversal of her natural intentions
to be gracious to inferiors and to protect her physical health.
She is shocked to have her condescension recognized and challenged

by the black woman who is her double. When she is knocked to the ground and both physically and psychologically "bruised" she realizes that her frequent phrase "the bottom rail is on the top" (p. 407) has become literally true. On the natural level she experiences society to be out of order. With the onset of her stroke, another order, the supernatural order, is revealed. Its meaning and values begin to be evident. Her earlier statements concerning the perversion of the social order have a bearing on her recognition at the close of the story, but they are the reverse of what she originally believed to be true. In other words, Julian's mother had correctly identified the essential problematic, namely the Black-White relationship in the social order and the question of her place in that order. However, through the in-breaking of grace, she is brought to realize that she herself is a proud, fallen and guilty woman. She cannot any longer depend upon her son, Julian, to protect her from this reality. In death, he is a stranger to her. She calls for her grandfather (Godhigh?) and her black nurse Caroline. The extent to which this is a retreat back to her childhood in the face of the total rejection of her operative world view as an adult or a response to the call to conversion ("unless you become like a little child") is unclear. Her spiritual destiny remains ambiguous.

Julian's mother is not typical of every O'Connor character depicted in Augustinian stories. First, it must be noted that though both she and Mrs. May ("Greenleaf") die immediately after the call to conversion, and as a result of the power of the grace-event, this is not an essential characteristic of these narratives. In the next chapter we will discuss *The Violent Bear It Away*, a story in which the protagonist's life continues after his call to conversion, now marked by a radical commitment to Christian prophecy. The mark of Augustinian stories is the call to conversion through the reversal of symbols and the recognition of it by a character, not the character's resulting death.

Nor is the apparent lack of acceptance of the call typical of this mode. Though Julian's mother cannot bear the revelation,

and seems closed to its implications, other characters have an
openness to grace which enables them to accept a change of heart
or conversion in this reversal situation. In such instances their
conversion involves an acceptance of the reversal of their intentions and the meaning of the symbols. They are in some way able
to integrate the new supernatural insight and the resultant conversion into their lives. For example, we have noted the response of Mrs. May in "Greenleaf." Though she too dies as the
result of her experience, her response in the moment of death
(Mr. Greenleaf sees her as bent over the bull "whispering some
last discovery into the animal's ear" [p. 334]) suggests at least
some acceptance of the call to conversion. An even clearer example will be noted in *The Violent Bear It Away*.

It is not the ultimate acceptance or rejection of the call
which is important to O'Connor; she refuses to pass final judgment on the eternal destiny of her characters. Nor is any such
final judgment essential to the classification of a story as Augustinian. What is essential is that the protagonist recognize
the action of grace as a reversal of previous symbols and intentions, which are now unmasked as sinful desires subject to the
concupiscence of fallen nature. The protagonist experiences this
opposition and unmasking as a call to conversion. This process,
present in the structure of "Everything That Rises Must Converge,"
is characteristic of Augustinian depictions of grace.

Jansenistic Grace: "Parker's Back"

O'Connor's descriptions of Jansenistic grace differ from
those we have just seen in that the opposition which grace brings
to nature now becomes an actual displacement. Sinful nature is
not only rejected and unmasked as corrupt; it is replaced by the
overwhelming power of grace. "Parker's Back" is an excellent example of this kind of portrayal.

Multivalent Symbols

The key symbol in "Parker's Back" is tattooing. The phenomenon of the tattoo is introduced at the beginning of the story where it has a single, literal meaning: a color mark or drawing on the skin.   At the outset of the story, then, the significance of the tattoo remains in the natural order. However, as the narrative develops, the symbol becomes highly specified and its natural significance is replaced by a supernatural meaning. In this kind of multivalent symbol, the original meaning of the symbol is not merely enhanced by the addition of a new meaning, nor is the original merely reversed. Rather, the original natural meaning is destroyed. In its place there is a new, totally different meaning.

Parker, the protagonist, is initially described by Flannery O'Connor as a youth who is "heavy and earnest, as ordinary as a loaf of bread" (p. 513). However, this nondifferentiated teenager experiences an "epiphany" while attending a town fair. In the side show he sees a tattooed man. "Except for his loins which were girded with a panther hide, the man's skin was patterned in what seemed from Parker's distance a single intricate design of brilliant color. The man, who was small and sturdy, moved about on the platform, flexing his muscles so that the arabesque of men and beasts on his skin appeared to have a subtle motion of its own" (pp. 512-513). Parker, for the first time in his life, if filled with emotion and awakened to an unexpected possibility. He beholds an ordinary man transformed into a thing of beauty. He too desires to become transformed.

Parker's quest for tattoos begins, but he is unable to understand fully the internal change which accompanies it. This first experience is so gentle and subtle that Parker is only partially aware of its significance. Having been gratuitously initiated into a metamorphic process, Parker is moved throughout the course of the story's development to acquire an ever increasing number of tattoos. The type of tattoo gradually progresses from pictures of inanimate objects such as anchors and cannons, through snakes, animals and birds, to drawings of Queen Elizabeth and Prince Phillip. At the same time that the type of object portrayed is becoming more developed in the scale of creation,

the internal drive toward gathering more tattoos is becoming an
uncontrollable obsession. As the tattoos increase, Parker begins
to decrease in personal significance.

When he is completely covered with drawings except for one
space in the center of his back, Parker experiences a second "e-
piphany." For some time, he has been experiencing a great sense
of dissatisfaction which initiates the quest for an additional
tattoo. However, this time the impulse is accompanied by the
feeling of an undefined but abiding presence. Then, one day when
he is at work baling hay near an ancient tree, the sun appears in
the burning sky and the tree seems to reach out and grab him.
His tractor hits a rock and he is thrown from it. The tractor
strikes the tree and both burst into flames. Parker sees his
shoes, which he has lost in the accident, consumed by the flames
and feels the "hot breath of the burning tree on his face" (p.
520).

Parker's response to this transformative experience is similar to his earlier reaction to the vision of the tattooed man at
the fair. He is unable to conceptualize what is happening to
him, but he realizes that the event is determinative for him.
"He only knew that there had been a great change in his life, a
leap forward into a worse unknown, and that there was nothing he
could do about it. It was for all intents accomplished" (p. 521).
At this point, Parker is merely continuing the process begun earlier, but now carried forward with burning intensity and great
speed. He has lost his ability to control any aspect of the
process. The burning of his shoes foretells the final burning
out of Parker himself.

He hurries to the tattoo parlor, aware that the final tattoo
which will take up the only remaining space must be one with religious significance. However, he is confident that when he
looks through the artist's book of pictures to be copied, the
right one will be manifest to him.

> He flipped the pages quickly, feeling that when he
> reached the one ordained, a sign would come. He contin-
> ued to flip through until he had almost reached the front
> of the book. On one of the pages a pair of eyes glanced

at him swiftly. Parker sped on, then stopped. His
heart too appeared to cut off; there was absolute
silence. It said as plainly as if silence were a language itself, GO BACK (p. 522).

Note how even the picture of the tattoo has a power over Parker.
He cannot resist it. His natural responses are stopped. He can
only obey and accept.

"Parker returned to the picture--the haloed head of a flat
stern Byzantine Christ with all-demanding eyes. He sat there
trembling; his heart slowly beginning to beat again as if it
were being brought to life by a subtle power" (p. 522). It is
consistent with the evolutionary development of the tattoo collection that Parker should be moved from the merely natural (created objects, animate and inanimate) level to the supernatural
(uncreated or divine) level. However, in this final overwhelming
action of grace, the remaining natural aspects of Parker himself
are displaced by the presence of the Christ symbolized in the
tattoo. He loses his personal identity. First his friends at
the pool hall and later his wife at home reject him. Their rejection is not personal, but is based solely on their refusal to
accept the Christ-sign Parker has become. He is expelled from
the pool hall and driven from his home. In the final scene, his
wife, Sarah Ruth, beats the Christ image on his back until the
face is bruised and swollen. Parker, stripped completely of his
personal identity and his previous life, including his wife and
friends, stands alone under a solitary tree, beaten and rejected.
He has become the sign of the suffering Christ he bears on his
back. The symbol of the Christ has displaced the natural man.
He is now a sign of the power of God over his creation.

Discrepancy in Action

As we noted in our discussion of symbols in "Parker's Back,"
the symbol of tattooing participates in the transformation of
meaning from the natural to the supernatural level. So, too, the
second literary device, discrepancy in action between intention
and outcome, portrays the transformation of the human action from
the natural outcome intended by the protagonist to a supernatural

outcome. This device is used in two related instances within the narrative: (1) Parker intends to transform himself into a work of art by collecting tattoos as had the tattooed man at the fair; and (2) Parker intends to please his wife, Sarah Ruth, by choosing as his final tattoo a religious drawing in order to assuage her claim that tattooing himself is an idolatrous act. In both instances, Parker's natural intention ceases. The outcome reveals a divine will which has intervened, replacing Parker's natural desire with a supernatural intention.

Parker collects tattoos because he wishes to emulate the beauty in design and color of the tattooed man at the fair. He intends his body to be naturally transformed through numerous colorful designs into a work of art. As he begins to collect various tattoos, he is dissatisfied. The effect is haphazard and unpleasant. His natural intention is not being fulfilled as he had intended. However, with the gathering of these first few tattoos, Parker becomes increasingly aware of a will other than his own which gradually overwhelms his power of self-determination. O'Connor has prepared the reader for this other intention from the outset of the tale. In recounting Parker's initial awakening at the sight of the tattooed man, O'Connor interjects the note that Parker felt something quicken inside him. He did not know what it was. As the story develops, this "other" force within Parker, which he experiences as a kind of drive or instinct to be followed but not understood, begins to manifest itself with increasing direction and power. The direction is not Parker's natural or intended direction, but another, completely different and incomprehensible. As this tattoo process develops, the inner drive becomes more absolute in its power over Parker. He is gradually diminished as it gains control over his actions.

As we noted above in our discussion of symbols in this story, much of the change in Parker comes through epiphanies which reveal directions and meanings, as in the case of the visions of the tattooed man and the burning tree. In each of these instances, Parker experiences an impulse which he blindly follows. Interwoven with the power of the divine directives are, at least

initially, Parker's own natural desires and intentions. But as
the power of divine grace increases, these desires cease and
his natural understanding of his actions and of the meaning of
symbols is displaced.

The process of displacement occurs mainly with regard to
Parker's relationship with Sarah Ruth. A large part of their
courtship and marriage is related to Parker's tattoos. He uses
them to attract her attention when they first meet. She is both
fascinated and repelled. Sarah Ruth is a biblical fundamentalist
who believes Parker's tattoos to be vain and sinful. Throughout
much of the story, Sarah Ruth tries to prevent Parker from obtaining more tattoos. She seeks to convert him from what she holds to
be his spiritual transgressions by refusing to look at his un-
clothed body in the light and by forbidding him to collect more
tattoos. She threatens him with a forecast of eternal damnation,
claiming that by his vanity he is "tempting sin" (p. 519).

Parker had not wanted to marry Sarah Ruth. He would have
preferred not to marry at all, but if he must have a wife, he
would have preferred a non-religious, earthy woman who appreciated
his tattoos. Despite his natural inclinations against Sarah Ruth,
he found himself impelled to marry her. Throughout the development of the story, Sarah Ruth and Parker struggle to change one
another. She seeks to save him; he searches for a tattoo that
will please her. Thus, the final tattoo, which will be placed in
the only uncluttered area, his back, must be especially suitable
to Sarah Ruth. Parker is cognizant of the fact that, because of
its location, he will be unable to see and enjoy the tattoo. Its
religious nature will therefore not disturb him and Sarah Ruth's
objection to the tattoos will be met.

This natural intention is intermingled with the drive toward
obtaining a final tattoo. The religious nature of the chosen
tattoo comes initially from Parker's natural intention and from
the divine demand made at the burning tree. However, when the
"eyes of the Byzantine Christ" make their demand known, Parker
comes more completely under the final transformative action of
grace. The Christ etched on his back begins to dominate the

situation. It takes on a lifelike quality which frightens the
boys at the pool hall and repels Sarah Ruth.

When Parker arrives home, Sarah Ruth is already angry. He
has been missing from both home and work during the two days that
it took to procure the intricate tattoo. She knows of the accident at work and that his employer expects to be repaid for the
loss of the tractor burned in the wreck. When Parker attempts to
explain that the "accident" has played a crucial role in the acquisition of this one final and surely most pleasing religious
tattoo, Sarah Ruth becomes even angrier. Viewing the head of the
Byzantine Christ tattooed on Parker's back as the most outrageous
form of idolatry, she drives him from her house, beating him on
the back with a broom as she expells him from her life.

Whereas Parker had intended by this tattoo to please Sarah
Ruth, he has completely alienated her. He, on the other hand,
had not expected to be personally affected by this tattoo in a
place invisible to himself, except insofar as it filled up the
last remaining space on his body. The picture to be placed on
his back had been of little interest to him, except that it would
satisfy his religiously obsessed wife. He did not intend that
the tattoo should change him. Even at the close of the story, he
does not understand the radical transformation which has taken
place in his life. Sarah Ruth's rejection of the Christ on his
back stops his action from reaching its intended natural outcome.

Instead, a supernatural intention dominates the scene. A
final transformation occurs which is so radical that everything
which has previously defined and described Parker is stripped
away or displaced. The face on his back literally takes over his
life. Parker himself is so battered, reduced and defeated that he
is unable to view his own transformation. He is left alone, an
exile from his former existence, "crying like a baby" (p. 530).
Stripped of his former self, he is reborn as a victim, a battered
and rejected Christ-type who is reduced to inaction. In this new
state, he is a mere victim-sign of the power of the divine intention.

Moment of Recognition

Because of the nature of the action of grace depicted in "Parker's Back," the recognition falls solely to the reader. The character of Parker, the human protagonist, has been so completely displaced through the workings of grace that he is literally no longer himself. This character has been so changed or burnt-out that only the outer shell of Parker remains. He has lost his job, his wife, his home, his shoes, his friends, and his personal identity. Stripped of his former life, he is denied by his friends and not only cast out but even beaten by his wife. This final action completes the transubstantiation begun through the gathering of the tattoos and continued through the acquisition of the last tattoo, that of the Byzantine Christ. Parker becomes the symbol on his back. At the conclusion of the story, he is a victim-sign, a suffering Christ-type. Since he is totally displaced by this new identity and his own natural actions have ceased, he is unable to participate in the cognition of the change which has taken place within him. He is discontinuous with his former self. Therefore, he is unable to re-cognize himself, even as changed. The displacement is complete. His rebirth is really his replacement by the tattoo.

Sarah Ruth, who in the story acts as Parker's antagonist, might have functioned, according to the type of grace portrayed, as a participant in the secondary recognition. However, she functions here as the final vehicle for the total transformation of Parker. In rejecting the Christ on his back, Sarah Ruth completes the meaning of the symbol, moving it from the natural to the supernatural level. She does not even experience Parker on the natural level as her husband who has acquired a new tattoo. Rather, she sees only the tattoo and she rejects its meaning. Her position is to deny completely the reality of the incarnation of Christ. Thus, in O'Connor's supernatural economy, Sarah Ruth herself commits the terrible error of rejecting a manifestation of the divine, the Christ-sign Parker has become. However, for the reader, her recognition of the natural state of Parker's return is an extremely important counterpoint. She completes Parker's

transformation into the Christ-sign when she rejects the face on
his back and viciously beats it. This act completes the displacement of the human character, reduces him further to inaction
and confirms the supernatural meaning of the symbol through its
rejection.

Primary recognition (recognition by the protagonist) is impossible due to the nature of the grace-act. And Sarah Ruth fails
to accept the true meaning of Parker's new tattoo. The recognition thus falls to the reader. The reader's recognition (tertiary recognition) is heightened by O'Connor's use of contrast
between Sarah Ruth's rejection of Parker and the obvious Christ-
symbols with which O'Connor describes Parker in the last scene.
O'Connor completes the Christ-identification of her protagonist:
"Parker was too stunned to resist. He sat there and let her beat
him until she had nearly knocked him senseless and large welts
had formed on the face of the tattooed Christ" (p. 529). Here
the author confirms for the reader Parker's total transmutation
into the symbol of the Christ. Grace has transubstantiated
Parker, displacing the natural for a supernatural significance.
In his displaced state, there is no "Parker" to recognize the
change. Hence the reader, in a tertiary recognition assisted by
Sarah Ruth's reaction and by O'Connor's description, supplies the
interpretation.

Jansenistic Grace: "The Comforts of Home"

Multivalent Symbols

The key symbol in "The Comforts of Home" is "home." At the
beginning of the narrative, this symbol has two natural meanings.
For Thomas, the protagonist,[6] it signifies his physical dwelling

---

[6]This story differs from "Parker's Back" and from most of
O'Connor's stories in that the "graced" character is not the
protagonist in the tale. Here there are two main characters,
Thomas and his mother. Grace acts on his mother through the central symbol in the story in a way similar to the action of grace
on Parker through his tattoos. Thomas' mother, like Parker, is

place where he enjoys physical comfort and freedom from pain and worry. For him, home refers to the well-ordered and pleasant life in his mother's house to which he is accustomed. For Thomas' mother, on the other hand, home is the heart or vital seat of life. It refers to an attitude of kindness, loving acceptance and the extension of this place of natural protection and conso- lation to others who have no physical or emotional home. For Thomas, then, the symbol is static, indicating a comfortable place to be preserved and maintained as one's due. For his moth- er, home refers more specifically to a dynamic situation requir- ing the exercise of a kind of familial generosity to those in need.

Throughout the development of the story, these two natural understandings of the symbol are in tension. In the action of grace, Thomas' mother's understanding of "home" is replaced by a supernatural meaning. Thomas' meaning, though not central to the action of grace in his mother's life, remains, though reject- ed, in order that the implications of the operation of grace on his mother might be more clearly demonstrated.

---

displaced by the action of grace, becoming a mere sign of the presence of God in the world.

But, unlike Parker, Thomas' mother is not the central char- acter or the protagonist from the literary perspective. Thomas plays this role, yet he is not the recipient of the graced ac- tion. Rather, Thomas serves as a counterface to the graced character, his mother. In this he is like Sarah Ruth in "Parker's Back." At the moment of grace, he is the antagonist through whom the final working of grace in his mother is accomplished. But he is the counterface to the graced character in even a more sig- nificant way. Throughout the development of the plot, he becomes, like his mother, driven by an unnatural force. But Thomas is compelled, not by divine grace, but by the power of the devil. Just as grace overwhelms his mother, replacing her with a sign of God's presence, so Evil, personified in the image of the "old man" (Thomas' dead father), becomes irresistible to Thomas. Thus Thomas serves as the diabolical antithesis to the action of grace. He too is displaced in the story, but by the power of Evil, not by the operation of grace. Since it is not our purpose here to examine the use of the demonic in O'Connor's work, but the oper- ation of grace, we will limit our consideration of Thomas to those aspects of his character and action which have a direct, if unwitting bearing on the actions of grace in the story.

Thomas' mother is a "good" woman who spends much of her
leisure time taking boxes of candy to neighbors and friends who
are ill. She naively assumes that all people are like herself
and her son, Thomas, basically "wholesome" people. Thus she believes that well-being, if temporarily lost, can be restored
through cheerfulness and kind gestures. At the beginning of the
story, she is moved to compassion by a newspaper account of a
nineteen year old girl, Sarah Ham, who is in prison for writing
bad checks. She sees Sarah as a wholesome-looking young woman
suffering hardship through her detention in a filthy jail. To
aid and comfort the girl, Thomas' mother proceeds to obtain a
lawyer as a consultant in the case, to have Sarah paroled to her,
and to find the young criminal a respectable place to live and
an honest job.

Thomas recognizes and appreciates his mother's domestic
kindness. He is accustomed to her habit of taking boxes of candy
to those needing cheer. When she decides to extend her generosity beyond its usual perimeters within her own social circle, to
a young woman in jail, he is amused. The thought of his mother
arriving there with a box of candy for a criminal strikes him as
rather ludicrous, but harmless. "Thomas was not cynical and so
far from being opposed to virtue, he saw it as the principle of
order and the only thing that made life bearable" (p. 386).
Thomas himself is dependent on his mother's sense of domestic
affections and orderly living. He enjoys the comfortable home
she makes for him. In fact, he expects as his due the well-ordered, but comfortable existence he experiences at his mother's
hand.

However, when his mother is drawn ever more significantly
into kind actions, Thomas begins to fear for his own comfortable
home. He realizes that "a moderation of good produces likewise
a moderation of evil" (p. 386). He expects and is willing to
tolerate some minor inconvenience in relation to his mother's
good deeds. But as she becomes more deeply involved in trying
to help Sarah Ham, a known liar and nymphomaniac, Thomas begins
to protest. When his mother brings the girl home to dinner after

her parole and later suggests that Sarah Ham (who calls herself Star Drake) might stay with them when she loses her job and lodging, Thomas realizes that his mother's kindness is endangering his own peaceful life. He begins to warn her that no excess of virtue can be justified and accuses her of "daredevil charity" (p. 383) which will destroy their home.

Thomas' mother is caught in the tension between Thomas' rational control, including even the regulation of virtue according to principles, and her own belief that Sarah Ham needs acceptance and a loving, secure home. Gradually her inability to change the girl's life (she has been called a "moral moron" by Thomas, and the lawyer claims that she is a psychopath, "not insane enough for the asylum, not criminal enough for the jail, not stable enough for society" [p. 388]) saddens the mother. She begins to compare Sarah Ham to her own son. He, for no discernable reason, had been born "fortunate," while this innocent child had been deprived of everything. As the extent of the girl's affliction and her own inability to alleviate it become evident, Thomas' mother is confronted with a deeper, painful mystery. An overbearing sense of discomfort and loss preoccupies her. She begins to identify Thomas in Sarah Ham as an unfortunate person who has no capacity for kindness or compassion. Gradually the two "children" become one image in her mind. "Her hazy charity no longer made distinctions" (p. 388).

When Sarah Ham attempts suicide and Thomas shows no sympathy for her, the weight of the mother's sorrow increases. She is "plunged into mourning for the world" (p. 397). The displacement of the symbol's meaning is nearly completed. The natural meaning of home as the vital center of human kindness and compassion is being replaced by the supernatural meaning of the symbol. The displacement is completed in the closing scene of the story. Thomas, trying to protect his home by killing Sarah Ham, mistakenly shoots his mother, who has been moved into the place of the girl. In her death, the supernatural meaning of the symbol is completed. Thomas' mother herself becomes displaced and identified with the suffering Christ who gives up his life (physical "home") to provide an everlasting home (eternal life) for others. Her natural kindness has been replaced by supernatural charity or complete self-sacrifice for others.

Discrepancy in Action

Thomas' mother intends merely to be kind to Sarah Ham, the young woman jailed for passing fraudulent checks. However, her actions do not yield the result she intends. Instead grace intervenes stopping the mother's action completely. Thomas' mother is burnt-out by the action of grace. She becomes unable to function as a person and a divine intention intervenes which determines the outcome of the narrative.

Thomas' mother's original intention is simply to visit the young woman and bring her some cheer. From the picture in the newspaper, Thomas' mother judges the girl to be less fortunate than she and her son. She goes to the jail, taking with her a box of candy for the girl, because it is a "nice thing to do" (p. 386). Becoming interested in the young woman's story and desiring to help her further, the mother returns to the jail a few days later, this time bringing some personal items and the promise of aid in obtaining a parole. Gradually Thomas' mother is impelled to extend her charity to the girl, Sarah Ham, beyond the limits of her original intention to "be nice." She begins to compare the comfortable situation of her son, Thomas, with the terrible plight of this young woman. As the comparison induces her to see major similarities in the two cases, she begins to be unable to distinguish the object of her kindness and her maternal drives. She begins to believe that Sarah Ham should share in all the security and material possessions which she had been able to provide for Thomas.

Though the girl consistently proves that she is socially unstable and emotionally disturbed, the mother is unable to control her loving acts. Thomas, ever increasingly upset at the major part the girl is beginning to play in his mother's life and concerned that Sarah Ham will ruin their home and living arrangement, tries to reason with his mother. He insists that she must take responsibility for her "daredevil charity" and that it must in this instance come to an end. However, his mother is by this time so consumed by her unlimited giving that she is unable to understand Thomas' concern in the matter. She has centered her attention and strength on Sarah Ham only in part intentionally. Her first steps, as we have noted, were based on the natural de- sire to be kind. However, the drive toward charitable action has carried her far beyond this original intention.

When Sarah Ham gets drunk and loses her job, Thomas' mother will not hear of having her sent back to jail. Rather, she im- pulsively rushes over to gather the girl's belongings from the boarding house which has evicted her and brings her home to their guest room. When the girl rushes nude into Thomas' room and he demands that she be sent away, his mother cannot think of such an unkind deed. Reacting to Thomas' "rejection" of her, Sarah Ham feigns a suicide attempt. Thomas demands that she be committed to the hospital where they have taken her for emergency treat- ment. Despite the indications that the continued acts of charity are destroying their home life--Thomas cannot and will not have his comfortable home existence further disrupted by Sarah--and despite the clear evidence that Sarah Ham will not respond to this loving environment--she goes to extremes to make life al- most unbearable--Thomas' mother seems unable to "listen to (nat- ural) reason." Even at the risk of losing her son and their re- lationship, she is unable to reject Sarah Ham. This total in- ability to make a considered judgment concerning her continued actions in Sarah's regard finally causes the mother's death.

The mother's charity has ceased to have meaning on the nat- ural level. Her acts are now unregulated and driven by the su- pra-human compulsion. What keeps the story from being the re- counting of the mother's psychotic illness caused by the overex- tension of her mental or emotional capabilities is that O'Connor carefully charts the mother's decline in proportion to her grow- ing identification with the suffering first of Sarah Ham, then of the world's poor and unfortunate, and finally of Christ Himself. At that moment, in making the final charitable gesture to protect

Sarah Ham from the bullet fired at her by Thomas, his mother per-
forms her final, supernaturally impelled act. It is an act of
total self-abnegation. She has given herself as a victim, en-
gulfed by the power of grace which displaces her totally. This
final moment serves as a sign of the power of divine charity in a
sinful world.

Moment of Recognition

In "The Comforts of Home," the recognition rests primarily
with the reader. Thomas' mother has been herself displaced by
the action of grace which she has experienced and is unavailable
to participate in its understanding. Neither Thomas, who fires
the shot intended for Sarah Ham which in fact kills his mother,
nor Sarah Ham herself, who has witnessed this last event, has any
reaction to the happenings here or any understanding of their
meaning. O'Connor records nothing of any of these characters except the account given by the sheriff whom Thomas has called.
Based on the evidence he sees, the sheriff assumes that Thomas
intended from the outset to kill his mother and attach the blame
for this action to the girl. The reader knows this to be an
ironic misreading of the situation.

The mother, who has experienced the operation of grace, has
been portrayed from early in the story's development as driven by
a type of charity which exceeds natural limits, including her own
intended involvement with Sarah Ham. The reader has seen how her
life is gradually taken over by this impulse, which blinds her to
the destruction of Thomas' life and her own. She mindlessly pur-
sues virtue until she makes a fool of herself and makes virtue
itself, at least from the human perspective, ridiculous. Thomas
has remarked accurately, if somewhat selfishly, that she has lost
the ability correctly to identify her actions and their results.
She is unable to distinguish Thomas, her own son, from the criminal she has taken in, who is systematically destroying the house
and Thomas' personal integrity as well as the orderly and naturally virtuous life which he and his mother have been living

together.

Thomas' mother's state after experiencing this action of grace is discontinuous with her former self. She has been burnt-out. Her natural virtues, including the ability to act reasonably and responsibly, and to recognize Thomas' human needs and respond to them lovingly, have been destroyed. She has been so displaced in her own life that she cannot cope with everyday chores, such as replacing the milk when it runs out. She cannot face the overwhelming evidence that Sarah is beyond "natural" help. Further, even when the helplessness of Sarah's case becomes glaringly evident to the point where Thomas' mother's own actions serve neither the girl nor anyone else, she impulsively carries on with a kind of mindless, driven charity. Thus, even before the shooting, Thomas' mother has become a burnt-out case, a suffering victim who bears witness to the power of God's grace in a fallen and corrupt world. Through the action of grace, she becomes a passive, impersonal type of the suffering Christ who gives Himself totally and indiscriminately to others.

This story is theologically different from other O'Connor narratives in which the protagonist dies in the end, such as "Greenleaf" of "Everything That Rises Must Converge," which have been discussed earlier, because here there is no real call to conversion. Thomas' mother, unlike Mrs. May and Julian's mother, does not participate knowingly in the final grace moment. She is not called to a supernatural understanding; her actions are not reversed or revealed as sinful. Rather, she herself is displaced. She has been burnt-out, and what remains after the action of this grace-event is not the original character, but a divine sign which bears witness to the presence of God.

These two stories, "Parker's Back" and "The Comforts of Home," depict a type of grace which, though similar to that which we have described in O'Connor's Augustinian narratives, differs markedly from it. In both stories the pivotal characters find themselves overwhelmed by the action of a grace so strong that it deprives them of their very personhood. Grace replaces nature.

CHAPTER THREE
VARIATIONS ON A THEME

The detailed analysis of the six stories in the previous chapter demonstrated how Flannery O'Connor employs several literary devices in patterned ways to create three different presentations of grace. In this chapter we shall examine three published versions of a *single* imaginative theme in order to demonstrate even more pointedly that O'Connor creates depictions of grace which range across a spectrum of understandings, presenting the operations of grace in different ways. These three variations on one theme show once again that there are distinct modes of grace portrayals in O'Connor's works. The analysis here, as in the previous chapter, will focus on the intrinsic process by which O'Connor combines differing modes of the three literary devices in her depiction of the workings of grace.

That Flannery O'Connor might combine various depictions of grace in reworking a single theme is not surprising. The operation of divine grace is the central focus of her writing. She was quite explicit about this. Indeed, in at least one story, "The Displaced Person," O'Connor included more than one type of presentation of grace within a single literary work. "The Displaced Person," which in its final form is a very long short story, is a composite of two shorter narratives.[1] In its original form, which included only the encounter between Mrs. Shortley, the resident farm worker, and Mr. Guizac, the "displaced person" who serves as a Christ-figure, the type of grace depicted is Augustinian. The second portion of the complete story, which adds the

---

[1] For a detailed discussion of the two parts of the story and an assessment of the relative merits of the two versions, see Male, "The Two Versions of 'The Displaced Person,'" pp. 450-457.

tale of Mrs McIntyre, the farm owner, presents a Jansenistic depiction of grace.[2] This combination of two different types of
portrayals within a single story contributes to the lack of integration which has been noted by critics.[3] Like the two novels,
this story is somewhat episodic, inferior in literary form and
technique to O'Connor's other short stories.

The core story which we will investigate in this chapter is
an initiation narrative. Its main characters are a young boy and
his older male teacher or guide. Each version is written in the
context of the relationship of nature and grace. The first variation, "The Artificial Nigger" (1955), depicts Thomistic grace,
and the second version, *The Violent Bear It Away* (1960), is an
Augustinian narrative. The third variation, "The Lame Shall
Enter First" (1962), differs from the three types we have previously examined in that it portrays more the absence than the presence of grace. This story bears some resemblance to both Augustinian and Jansenistic narratives. Yet it moves beyond these
modes to utilize the three literary devices in such a way as to
present a grace narration analogous to a Manichaean approach to
God and nature.

Though it is tempting to suggest a linear development in
O'Connor's theology of grace based on the knowledge that she published the Thomistic story first, then worked for several more
years on the second version which portrays an Augustinian concept
of grace, and then shortly thereafter published the Manichaean
one, such a theory of theological development is not warranted,
for at least two reasons: (1) study of other stories according to
their theological content and publishing dates gives no evidence
of such an evolution, and (2) recent research on early O'Connor
manuscripts indicates that substantial portions of "The Lame
Shall Enter First" appear as early as and in some cases in

---

[2]As shown by an analysis of the use of literary devices similar to that found in this study.

[3]See, for example, Bornhauser, "Review of *A Good Man Is Hard
to Find*," p. 77.

conjunction with the material used in "The Artificial Nigger."[4] We must assert, rather, from the evidence of these three texts themselves and from the structurally different concepts of grace depicted throughout the O'Connor corpus that Flannery O'Connor did not move toward an emphasis on any one concept of grace in her fiction, but rather explored the imaginative possibilities of different understandings of the grace-event. We will seek to demonstrate this through an examination of the thrice-told tale: "The Artificial Nigger," *The Violent Bear It Away*, and "The Lame Shall Enter First."

The three stories (actually a short story, a novel and a novella) are related in numerous ways. As Dunn points out in his study of the early manuscripts, much of the material passed back and forth between the versions, especially with regard to *The Violent Bear It Away* and "The Lame Shall Enter First."[5] Both of these works were published in final form long after the publication of "The Artificial Nigger." They are also much more detailed and longer pieces of fiction. As Dunn suggests, it is not possible to determine which elements were originally intended as parts of which variation. The early manuscripts show much interchange.[6] The three variations are interrelated in complicated and overlapping ways and the original manuscripts cannot all be accurately dated. It is sufficient here to note the complexity of the issue and to understand that in many senses all three of these published works were at one time part of the same imaginative theme.

Our first task is to discuss the relationships between these three works. The clearest way to do this is by making two separate comparisons based on the most obvious connections between the stories: first, between "The Artificial Nigger" and *The*

---

[4]Dunn, "The Manuscripts of Flannery O'Connor at Georgia College," pp. 65-67; and Asals, "Hawthorne, Mary Ann, and 'The Lame Shall Enter First,'" pp. 4-6.

[5]Dunn, "The Manuscripts," p. 66.

[6]Dunn, p.67.

Violent Bear It Away, and second, between *The Violent Bear It
Away* and "The Lame Shall Enter First." The relationships can be
seen most clearly in this way because the second work, *The Violent Bear It Away*, incorporates most directly elements found in
the other two variations. Perhaps for this reason this novel is
among O'Connor's least tightly structured works.

   We will discuss only the final published version of each
work in order to demonstrate that O'Connor reworked these materials in such a way as finally to create out of a single, complicated narrative three different stories, each depicting a different concept of the actions of grace.

   We have already described and analyzed "The Artificial Nigger." *The Violent Bear It Away*, especially in its first part, is
closely parallel. Both stories are based on a journey motif.
The main characters are similarly described by O'Connor and have
similar familial relationships to one another. In both stories
an old man and his young male relative are brought to a deeper
knowledge of the world's religious meaning.

   In the first story, the two characters, Mr. Head and Nelson,
are grandfather and grandson. In the second story, the relationship is changed to great-uncle and grand-nephew and expanded to
include the boy's uncle and this uncle's retarded son. In many
ways, the two adult men in *The Violent Bear It Away* can be seen
as aspects of the single character, Mr. Head; and similarly, the
two youths can be seen as aspects of Nelson. In naming her characters, O'Connor suggests allusion to the Apostle Peter in the
New Testament. In "The Artificial Nigger," the grandfather is
called Mr. Head, a reference to Peter as "head" of the Church,
its authority and leader; in *The Violent Bear It Away*, the great-
uncle is called Mason Tarwater, again a Petrine reference, this
time to the "mason" who works in rock.

   In both stories there is a trip to Atlanta. The city serves
as a symbol of evil. In the first story the journey is taken by
Mr. Head and Nelson. It forms the central theme of the story and
is a major vehicle for the development of the plot. Mr. Head has
planned the journey to teach Nelson about the evils of the world,

especially the existence of "niggers" and the danger in failing to recognize them. In the second narrative, reference is made to a trip to the city taken earlier by Mason and the boy, Francis Marion Tarwater. After the death of Mason Tarwater, the youth makes the second trip alone. His purpose, like the Heads', is to gain knowledge. In both stories the outcome of the journey differs from its original intention. However, as was noted in the last chapter, in the first story the action of grace is portrayed in a Thomistic way, and the outcome builds on and enhances Mr. Head's intention. In the second story, which is Augustinian, the outcome is reversed in keeping with the supernatural design. We will return to this in more detail later in the chapter.

Certain of the symbols used in *The Violent Bear It Away* recall those of the shorter "The Artificial Nigger." In that story the "nigger" is a complex symbol whose function is to reunite the opposites created through the unfolding of the plot. The central focus of the grace-event in the story, the plaster statue of the black man eating a piece of watermelon, ironically unites age and youth, black and white, defeat and victory, evil and goodness. According to Dunn, the original draft for *The Violent Bear It Away* included an encounter between the two Tarwaters and a watermelon-eating black man just after the older Tarwater's denial of the younger one. However, this encounter, according to Dunn, has no "epiphanic impact."[7] In the final version of this second story, the figure of the "nigger" is in part replaced by two other characters: Bishop, the "idiot" son who bears the suffering, old man image; and the "stranger" who personifies the dark, evil aspects of the "nigger." Other symbols are also used in the later, longer version. Fire and water images are of central significance. These symbols are used to demonstrate the oppositional relationship of nature and grace which typifies O'Connor's Augustinian stories.

The second and third variations of the narrative, *The*

---

[7]Dunn, "The Manuscripts," p. 66.

Violent Bear It Away and "The Lame Shall Enter First," present
even more points of similarity than do the first and second.   In
both of these versions O'Connor expands her basic character types
and develops further lines of action, moving away from the relative simplicity of "The Artificial Nigger."

Corresponding to Mason Tarwater in *The Violent Bear It Away*
(and to Mr. Head in "The Artificial Nigger") is Rufus Johnson's
absent but hauntingly powerful grandfather.   Though he does not
actually appear in "The Lame Shall Enter First," his influence on
young Rufus, a "religious" juvenile delinquent with a club foot,
is quite as certain and as ultimately compelling as that of Mason
Tarwater on young Francis Marion.

In both the second and third versions of the story, a second
adult male character is introduced.   In both cases he is central
to the story's development.   In *The Violent Bear It Away* the man
is Rayber, uncle to young Tarwater and father to a retarded son,
Bishop.   In "The Lame Shall Enter First," the figure is Sheppard,
counsellor at the reformatory where Rufus Johnson has been imprisoned.   He too has a son, Norton, whom he believes to be
"morally retarded."   Both men profess a sort of secular humanism
and are employed in a helping profession.

Rayber is a teacher who has previously made a conscious decision to reject the fundamentalist religion of his uncle, Mason
Tarwater, and, therefore, to prevent the baptism of his son,
Bishop.   Rayber is now developing an educational theory based on
secular humanism.   He believes that through rationalism and asceticism human persons can avoid both God and sin.   However, in
the outcome of the story, he is stripped of his sterile intel-
lectualism.   His mentally retarded son is rudely taken from his
custody both spiritually and physically.   Bishop is baptized and
drowned.

A parallel situation is portrayed in "The Lame Shall Enter
First."   Sheppard is a volunteer social worker at the reformatory.   He too is a secular humanist, although he seems not to
have consciously thought out his philosophy.   Throughout the development of the narrative, his religious stance is challenged by

his son, Norton, who desires a religious explanation of his mother's death, and by Rufus Johnson, the biblical fundamentalist delinquent he befriends and tries to help. In the final scene Sheppard's son is dead by suicide and the delinquent is on his way back to the reformatory. Sheppard has failed both as a father and as a counsellor. For reasons which will be discussed later, his position is more tragic than is Rayber's in that he has lost the possibility of change. The vehicles for his acceptance of grace, Norton and Rufus, are both gone. With Rayber, on the other hand, there is some hint that the God/love he has sought to resist is now free to act upon him.

In both of these stories, a dead or absent older prophet haunts the action and the lives of the characters. The secular humanists resist them, but the young truth seekers accept them literally (albeit not without a struggle), ultimately recognizing their prophecy as closer to truth than the atheistic position of the "professional humanizers." The tension in both stories is created by the conflict between the two worlds projected by the adults. In *The Violent Bear It Away*, Francis Marion Tarwater must set some course for himself. He has two options: the prophetic role assigned him by his great-uncle Mason, or the atheistic position offered him by his uncle Rayber. In "The Lame Shall Enter First," Rufus Johnson has already begun a destructive life of crime. He is caught in the tension between a secular savior and the biblical understanding of the mercy of Jesus taught him by his grandfather.

In both stories, the action centers around the "do-gooder's" son. In *The Violent Bear It Away*, the child is a five-year-old "idiot." Tarwater and Rayber battle over the child's destiny and the meaning of his human existence. In "The Lame Shall Enter First," the child is an eleven-year-old "moral moron." In both cases, the child's "salvation" is expressed in opposing possibilities: the secularist proposes a humanistic approach (in the case of the retarded child, the condition is viewed as a fate to be coped with; in the case of the selfish, immoral child, the appeal is to some higher set of values within); the religious zealot, not

himself truly converted, proposes death for each. In both instances, death assumes a proportion unsuspected by either of the
parties involved in the power struggle over the life of the
child.

   The three variations are not identical, but they share many
aspects of plot, character and theme. The first version, like
the later two, concerns a youth who seeks truth under the direction or influence of a fundamentalist patriarch. All three variations include trips to or life within the city, which is a sign
of evil. The city has the power to corrupt, to draw the believer
away from Truth. Each version includes denial or desertion of
the young man by his prophetic relative and the youth's final acceptance of the religious values espoused by the prophet. The
two later variations add two characters who serve as counter-
points to the prophet and youth. The secular humanist tries to
save the youth from what he perceives to be the absurdity and
self-destruction of prophetic fundamentalism. And each of the
humanists is father to a son whose untimely death is caused by
the action or influence of the prophet-haunted youth.

   Yet despite this similarity of character, plot and situation, each variation is significantly different from the others.
The difference lies not in the external elements but in the concept of grace which O'Connor portrays in each version. By her
skillful use of varying modes of literary devices and by combinations of these, she depicts operations of grace which differ theologically from one another.

The First Variation: "The Artificial Nigger"

   Because this story was discussed at length in the last chapter, we need only recall the important aspects of that study. As
we have noted, in "The Artificial Nigger" O'Connor employs various literary devices to depict Thomistic grace.

   O'Connor employs multivalent symbols, including the central symbol of the "nigger," to unite the elements of the story
which have been disjoined through the person's alienation from
God, self and nature. The symbol of the "nigger" gradually gains

meaning, expanding to hold in creative tension the disparate elements presented as aspects of the fallen world reunited in the moment of grace. The plaster statue of the Negro contains symbolic components of age and youth, black and white, suffering and glory. None of these elements is reversed or rejected. They continue to exist, but now in the creative tension that enables the human person, aided by this unifying and completing grace, to carry on his or her life in a world fallen, but not depraved. Nature is not scorned, but uplifted by God in his merciful intervention.

A second literary device employed to portray Thomistic grace in this story is discrepancy in action between intention and outcome. We recall that Mr. Head intended to teach Nelson to identify "niggers," to recognize the evil and danger of the city, and to acknowledge his grandfather's wisdom. These intentions are achieved in the moment of grace, when the statue appears gratuitously to reunite the Heads and to re-establish their relationship. In addition, Mr. Head experiences forgiveness for his sin of pride and the comfort of divine mercy. His knowledge of reality is corrected and enhanced. The divine outcome is superior, even by Mr. Head's own admission, to that of his intended plan. The outcome is not a reversal, but an enrichment, a perfection of the human intention.

A third literary device noted in this story is the moment of recognition. Both Nelson and Mr. Head participate in a new awareness. Between the two characters there is a mutual recognition of guilt and forgiveness. Their relationship to one another is first re-established and then enhanced through their encounter with the "artificial nigger." Mr. Head undergoes a further recognition that his personal guilt has been forgiven. He understands now that he is a part of the sinful, fallen world, a totally new insight for the man who had proudly asserted his own perfection and independence from the rest of humankind. Yet, despite this, he has been granted God's mercy. Again, grace and nature are reunited. Mr. Head understands the insight he has been granted, acknowledges its divine source, and is able to

Admit both his own need and the total gratuity of the grace. He
realizes that he has not merited in any way the mercy he now experiences.

The first variation, "The Artificial Nigger," thus uses the
literary devices of multivalent symbols, discrepancy in action,
and moment of recognition in their first modes. The result is
a story which presents a Thomistic approach to the operation of
grace.

The Second Variation: *The Violent Bear It Away*

The second version of the story, a novel entitled *The Violent Bear It Away*, depicts a presentation of grace which suggests
analogy to Augustinian thought. As a novel the work suffers from
some disunity and from a failure of artistic imagination.[8] However, our interest here centers not on the novel's technical and
artistic merits, but on its portrayal of a type of grace-event
substantially different from that found in the story's first and
third versions.

In *The Violent Bear It Away*, O'Connor uses the same literary
devices as in her shorter fiction. She employs the devices of
multivalent symbols, discrepancy in action between intent and

---

[8]See, for example, Creekmore, "A Southern Baptism," pp. 20-
21; and Drake, "Miss O'Connor and the Scandal of Redemption," p.
430. In addition to her thirty-one short stories, O'Connor wrote
two novels and left a brief sketch of a third. Her novels have
generally been viewed as inferior to her short stories (see the
examples cited above, p. 2, n. 2). Some critics, including
Asals, "Flannery O'Connor as Novelist," pp. 23-39; Rubin, "Flannery O'Connor and the Bible Belt," p. 51; and Stephens, *The Question of Flannery O'Connor*, pp. 43-45, suggest, however, that the
novels, though flawed and lacking in the artistic excellence of
many of the short stories, are nonetheless impressive in their
own right and warrant more serious critical consideration than
they have usually received. One critic believes *The Violent Bear
It Away* to be O'Connor's best work (Hyman, "Flannery O'Connor,"
p. 345). Stephens argues that the novels contain some of O'Connor's best writing, especially the last chapter of *Wise Blood* and
the first two chapters of *The Violent Bear It Away* (*The Question
of Flannery O'Connor*, p. 43).

outcome, and the moment of recognition in much the same way as in her Augustinian short stories. Whenever a literary device is used in protray this type of grace, some reversal of meaning is entailed.

Multivalent Symbols

The literary device of multivalent symbols to depict in the novel an Augustinian concept of grace occurs in two ways: (1) a single symbol reveals two opposed meanings, one of which is apparent until it is reversed in the moment of grace, or (2) two symbols whose meanings are opposed coexist in the story until the moment of grace affirms one and denies the other.

Fire is an example of a single symbol used in the novel which carries two opposed meanings. Initially fire indicates destruction and evil. The old prophet, Mason Tarwater, fears that his rationalistic nephew, Rayber, will dispose of his body at the old man's death by burning it rather than by giving it a Christian burial. Burning with fire here indicates a secular understanding of the body as refuse to be disposed of efficiently. He thus charges his grand-nephew with conducting a proper burial. When the old man dies, young Tarwater, after a half-hearted attempt to dig a grave, does set fire to the house containing the body. The fire is intended to consume the body and for the young Tarwater it is a symbol of self-determination in the face of a religious mandate to provide a Christian burial for the old prophet. Once Tarwater has left the site of the burning house and started toward the city, he identifies the city lights with the fire he has just set. Symbolically he moves from the destruction for which he is responsible to the larger evil and destruction of the city.

At the end of the initial journey, after he has been raped and stripped both literally and symbolically of his self-identity and pride, Tarwater again lights a fire in the woods of his homestead. However, this fire has the reverse meaning and effect of the first one he had lit in the same place. Now the fire symbolizes the purging of the evil and the destructive ways of humankind.

It takes on the significance of a divine act which defeats the
evil forces in the woods and drives out the evil with Tarwater. Thus, in one instance, fire is malevolent; in the second
instance, after the moment of grace, it is benevolent in its purgation. Through the action of grace of the second type of fire,
Tarwater is converted from the ways of the devil to the ways of
the Lord. Whereas the fire symbol first indicated the reign of
destruction in the land, in the reversal of the symbol, fire
comes to indicate the reign of divine mercy through purgation.

Like fire, water is a central symbol which bears a double
meaning. In the novel, water connotes both death and life. The
old prophet has given young Tarwater the task of baptizing the
"idiot" child Bishop. Although at first Tarwater tries to ignore
the child and to omit the task, he finds the child compelling and
the constant proximity of water (fountains in the park, the lake
in the center of the woods, etc.) unnerving. Thinking himself
unable to withstand the internal and external pressures to bap-
tize the child, Tarwater decides to drown him instead.

Rayber, Bishop's father, believes that taking the boys away
from the pressures of the city to the lake for the weekend will
have a calming effect on Tarwater and distract him from his obsession with the child. In fact, the lake water violently at-
tracts both boys and provides Tarwater the opportunity to accomplish his purpose: to prevent himself from baptizing the child by
killing him instead. He does drown Bishop. The water fulfills
its destructive function. Not only is the troublesome child
dead, but the hated role of prophet is laid aside. The meaning of
water in this act is that of consuming and extinguishing life.
However, as the act is nearly completed, grace intervenes. Tarwater "accidently" pronounces the words of baptism over the
drowning child. The water of death becomes the water of spiritual life. The meaning of the symbol is reversed. What initially
symbolized and provided the vehicle for the accomplishment of the
sinful, rebellious act of murder now symbolizes and becomes the
vehicle for the saving act of baptism.

An example of a pair of symbols which coexist throughout the

novel until the moment of grace when the meaning of one is affirmed and the other is denied is found in the contrasting world
views of Rayber and Old Tarwater, the prophet. Rayber's attitude
symbolizes the position of mechanistic rationalism. He is a secular humanist who approaches reality, both in his professional
life as a teacher and in his private life as the father of Bishop, his mentally retarded son, from the viewpoint that the person
is capable of shaping his or her destiny and is solely responsible for it. He explains the condition of his son as an accident of nature which is regrettable, but unavoidable. Old Tarwater's attitude, on the other hand, symbolizes the position of
the literal believer. He is a biblical fundamentalist, a prophet
whose message of God's universal wrath and whose personal wres-
tlings with the Lord are the essential elements in life.

Young Tarwater, at the opening of the story, decides against
what seems to be the religious fanaticism of the old prophet and
the unreasonable prophetic tasks left unfinished at the prophet's
death. When he sets out for Rayber's house in the city, his purpose is to examine Rayber's understanding of the meaning of life.
He is prepared to accept Rayber's philosophy to the extent that
it seems "right." He is quickly able, however, to discard mechanistic rationalism as false and shallow. Tarwater chooses to
develop some moderate stance between the opposing symbolic systems. But no compromise is possible. Opposites are absolute in
O'Connor's Augustinian works. What may appear reasonable to the
reader, namely, secular humanism, is shown to be unreasonable in
the moment of grace when Rayber's world view is rejected.

Tarwater thus experiences a reversal in the meaning of the
symbol. He undergoes a conversion which reveals to him the real
wisdom of the old prophet. The position he originally denounced
becomes his own, willingly accepted in the light of the grace-
event. The reader also experiences a reversal of meaning.
Throughout the novel, despite its shortcomings in practice, Rayber's philosophy has symbolized an understanding of modern life
seemingly far more balanced and reasonable than that asserted by
the old prophet. Thus young Tarwater experiences a reversal in

the meaning of the symbol systems when he realizes that Rayber's position has been invalidated and rejected in the action of grace.

The second pair of symbols which coexist throughout the work until the moment of grace are birth and rebirth. Here the symbols are almost literal and O'Connor does not integrate them well into the novel. Tarwater's birth, an illegitimate and unprepared event which takes place at the scene of an automobile crash, symbolizes the unfortunate, even catastrophic condition of the human person at birth. Natural birth holds no hope. Rayber claims, however, that it also reveals the truth about the person. One is abandoned to oneself and must struggle against the forces of nature to survive. To set one's hopes on the mystery, miracle and authority of religion is to deceive oneself and degrade the dignity of humankind.

Rebirth, specifically experienced here in baptism, entails according to Tarwater life in the ways of the Lord. Despite the hardship and demands caused by serving the Lord, this is the only way to prepare for the true life which is the supernatural existence of the next world. The meanings of birth and rebirth are discussed theoretically by Rayber and Tarwater at the beginning of the work. However, only as the narrative develops do the symbols gradually gain meaning until the climactic realization in the series of grace-events which Tarwater undergoes. At the culmination of these events, he recognizes the reversal of meanings. Rebirth becomes for him the only significant event. Through its acceptance, he comes to acknowledge his special significance in the divine economy.

Discrepancy in Action

The second literary device which O'Connor uses to portray the Augustinian concept of grace in *The Violent Bear It Away* is discrepancy in action between intention and outcome. This device is an important literary vehicle for the expression of Augustinian grace, which reverses human intention to reveal the plan of divine providence. The discrepancy appears often throughout the narrative, but it is most significant in Tarwater's decision to reject his two divinely assigned tasks during his initiation as prophet of God.

From the outset of the story, Tarwater recognizes the nature and scope of the two deeds which he is required to perform: (1) the Christian burial of the dead prophet, including the digging of a ten foot deep grave and the erection of a cross (to be gathered by the angels on Judgment Day) at the head of the grave, and (2) the baptism of his retarded cousin, Bishop. Tarwater first rejects the tasks as beneath the dignity of a real prophet. He looks forward to achieving something more spectacular in the name of the Lord. He is initially willing to perform either significant tasks or else no prophetic tasks at all. He refuses to carry out these charges, which he believes to be inconsequential. As the plot develops, Tarwater begins to assert himself more specifically against the divine requirements set down for him through his great-uncle, the old prophet. Defiantly, he chooses a course of action based simply on his own integrity and self-reliance.

Tarwater's first act of independence concerns the burial of the old prophet. He reluctantly begins the task and digs through the sandy topsoil without difficulty. By the time he strikes rock, he is tiring. He begins to consider that his uncle, Rayber, who has cast aside both his baptism and its religious regulations and presuppositions, would dispose of the body by burning it, a meaningless but efficient method of dealing with the problem. Finally Tarwater abandons his task temporarily to refresh himself with the old prophet's forbidden stash of homemade liquor. He falls into a drunken stupor. A black neighbor who comes to replenish his own supply of liquor finds the body of the dead man in the house and reproves the boy for failing in his Christian duty to bury the body properly and for getting drunk. Tarwater continues to drink until he passes out. When he awakens, it is nightfall. By this time, he has decided not to complete the burial as he has been instructed, but rather to incinerate the body by burning down the house in which he believes it still

rests. After setting the fire, he leaves the property, convinced
that he has successfully resisted the first task. He has acted
in direct contradiction to the requirement by burning, not burying the body and by failing to erect a cross to mark the grave
for the resurrection of the last day. Not until the completion
of his journey to the city and the baptism/drowning of Bishop
does Tarwater return to the place to discover that the outcome of
his action is the reversal of his intention. Seeing him too
drunk to complete the burial, the black man has undertaken the
task himself. The grave is complete with the cross at its head.

The second use of the literary device of discrepancy in action between intention and outcome is a more direct and exacting
depiction of the reversal entailed in the Augustinian concept of
grace. Once in the city, and having examined his own position in
relation to Rayber's philosophy of mechanical rationalism, Tarwater decides once again, but this time more consciously, to act
in order to gain his freedom and to determine his own future.
Faced with the constant danger of baptizing the "idiot" child due
to their mutual attraction to one another and the child's compul-
sive drive toward bodies of water, and with the haunting dread
of the unaccomplished task, Tarwater decides to drown the child.
His intention is twofold: (1) to end the risk of unwittingly performing the required baptism, and (2) to assert his choice for an
independent future apart from the power of his dead uncle, the
old prophet, and his prophetic destiny. Thinking of his state
after the murder, he fantasizes: "Now I can do anything I want"
(p. 317). He has discounted the power of the divine intention
and the possibility of the intrusion of grace.

As he initiates the murderous act by plunging Bishop's head
under the surface of the lake, the child violently resists and
struggles for survival. In the physical conflict for power over
the situation, Tarwater "accidentally" says the words of baptism
over the drowning child. The action is completed, but its outcome is the reverse of his intention. The murder has become an
act of salvation. Ironically, it is not the "idiot" child who is
saved, but Tarwater. The child is described throughout the

narrative as a primitive innocent. Incapable of human action, including sin, he does not require a personal act of redemption. Tarwater, on the other hand, has directly contravened the divine will on two accounts. He has committed murder and in so doing has rejected the divine imperative for him. He has attempted to assert his own sinful will. But grace intervenes. The moment becomes an epiphany for him. The divine will has intervened to reverse the meaning of the human action.

In the development of the novel, a sequence of events further prepares and purifies Tarwater, enabling him to begin to understand the meaning of his own earlier, but rejected baptism. God has a design for him, a further task. Not until he returns home to discover the contravention and reversal of his attempt to escape the appointed task of burying his great-uncle does he fully realize the implications of the epiphany moment at the lake drowning. He has undergone a radical conversion. Now he is prepared to accept his final task, the proclaiming of the "terrible mercy of God" to the sinful city.

Moment of Recognition

There are numerous instances of insight or recognition throughout the novel. Three are of specific concern to our study because they depict a series of events which culminate in the final conversion of the protagonist, Tarwater. As the narrative develops, Tarwater makes a series of choices and undergoes a sequence of reversals which gradually reveal to him his own fallen condition and the possible supernatural direction of his life. In each of these instances, Tarwater experiences some correction of his erroneous understanding of himself and the reversal of his original intention. The recognition of the reversal is the key element used to depict the meaning of the series of actions and their outcomes.

The first moment of recognition takes place at the drowning/ baptism of Bishop. Tarwater recognizes that some force outside of his control, namely grace, has intervened to reverse the meaning

of his action. The murder has become not only a death-event
but also a life-event. The act has ended Bishop's worldly existence.[9] It also radically affects Tarwater and Rayber. Tarwater
recognizes that the intention of his action has been reversed.
The task he rejected he has done. The child is baptized.
Against his own desire, he has successfully completed the deed,
although not as the old prophet had described it. This recognition, however, is only partial. Although the baptism has oc-
occurred, it has not been willed by Tarwater and he as succeeded in
killing the child. He takes some comfort in the murder of Bishop
and hopes that his own intention is sufficient to counteract the
effect of the baptismal words he has accidentally spoken.

The second moment of recognition, again a reversal, involves
the unmasking of a minor character. Throughout the narrative,
beginning at the death of the old prophet, Tarwater has been vi-
sited by a "stranger" who takes various forms. He is presented
first as a voice which encourages Tarwater to burn his great-uncle's body rather than continuing the difficult physical labor of
burying him. The voice also encourages Tarwater to set his own
course in opposition to those set down for him by the old prophet
and his uncle Rayber. He suggests that Tarwater resolve his dilemma concerning his second task by drowning the child. At the
actual drowning, the stranger again appears as a voice which encourages Tarwater to complete the task.

Once the task, including the baptism, is completed, however,
the voice begins to mock Tarwater and undermine his confidence in
having chosen a separate and independent path. Until this time

---

[9]The murder of Bishop seems of little consequence in moral
terms. The commission of a murder first confirms Tarwater in
evil and then the same act frees him to begin doing good, to
undertake the prophetic tasks which will be assigned for the salvation of the rest of the world, symbolized by the evil city. In
many ways, Bishop is the innocent victim whose death is an expia-
tion for the world. Concerning the impact of the murder on Tarwater's own moral and spiritual condition, O'Connor writes in a
letter to a friend: "That murder is forgotten by God and of no
interest to society" (*Habit of Being*, p. 343).

in the narrative, the stranger has been portrayed as an alter
ego, a friend and confidant to Tarwater. However, once the conversion process begins in the grace-event at the lake, the stranger begins to change. He becomes mildly hostile. Tarwater puts
the stranger's voice out of his mind as he flees the baptism/
drowning scene. As he walks toward his now burnt-out home, he is
tired, thirsty, but preoccupied with the meaning of the recent
event. On the way he is picked up by a passing motorist and offered a ride. The motorist seems kind, and Tarwater is grateful
for the unsolicited help. He offers Tarwater a drink from his
liquor supply in the car's glove compartment. The boy finds the
stranger vaguely familiar, but he is tired and the liquor quickly
reduces him to a drunken stupor. The stranger pulls the car off
the road, rapes the drunken boy, steals his few possessions and
leaves him naked in the woods.

When Tarwater awakens, he recognizes first his violated
state, and then the similarities between this stranger who appeared to befriend him, but in fact victimized him, and the earlier stranger. He now realizes that the first stranger, too, had
victimized him by manipulating him in such a way that he would
ultimately meet defeat at the hands of the divine. Now he understands that the two strangers are in reality one. The stranger
is an evil character who, despite his own demonic ways, moves the
divine plan forward. In this second use of the literary device
of the moment of recognition, the awareness is again that of a
reversal. The one whom Tarwater believed to be his friend is revealed, through the violent action of rape, to be the enemy.
Once again the moment of recognition is a reversal which is accompanied by a change in Tarwater's own state. This time the reversal is both physical and emotional.

The third moment of recognition occurs when Tarwater reaches
the homestead. He has set fire to the woods where he was raped
to indicate his rage and to set a symbolic wall of fire between
himself and the friend/enemy. On reaching the homestead, two re-
alizations come upon him: (1) he has, in fact, been raped on his
own land, and (2) the old prophet has, indeed, received a full

Christian burial. His intention has been reversed. The black
neighbor has intervened to save the body from the burning house
and has completed the task of burying the old man. As Tarwater
stares in shocked disbelief at the cross marking the grave, he
becomes aware of the wall of flames advancing toward him from the
fire he has set in the woods. He interprets the fire to be the
same fire that encircled Daniel and raised the prophet Elijah
from the earth. Throwing himself on the grave, he again hears a
strange voice. This time, he recognizes it to be of divine origin. The voice commands him to return to the city to "warn the
children of God of the terrible speed of mercy" (p.447). Following this final moment of conversion, Tarwater's "singed eyes,
black in their deep sockets, seemed already to envision the fate
that awaited him as he moved steadily on, his face set toward
the dark city, where the children of God lay sleeping."

* * *

As was noted earlier, the novel is episodic and the literary
devices are not used as skillfully in this work as they are in
other stories of the same type. In several shorter Augustinian
works, the concept of the power of grace as the reversal of the
human in the light of the divine is far more effective artisti-
cally. Yet *The Violent Bear It Away* is clearly an attempt to
portray the Augustinian concept of grace. The literary devices
employed in the novel each function, if not with complete effec-
tiveness, in the same manner as in the short stories of the same
type. The meaning of the key symbols is reversed, the protagonist sees his intention rejected in the outcome of his action,
and the moment of recognition entails the recognition of a call
to conversion by the protagonist, who thereby undergoes a change
in his condition.

The novel suffers from structural weaknesses. Both the
black neighbor and the stranger appear, affect the outcome of the
action, and vanish. They are not sufficiently integrated into
the fabric of the novel to participate so profoundly in the development of the narrative. Each is a *deus ex machina*, a mere

vehicle. The third moment of recognition is so complex and detailed as to lose the effect of its power of reversal. O'Connor
seems to use it to resolve the many conflicts and loose ends
which ought to have been resolved elsewhere. Finally, as we can
observe from our brief description of some of the content entailed in the final moment of recognition, O'Connor falls into
the trap of didacticism. Evidence of this can be found in certain segments of the dialogue between Tarwater and both of his
uncles. For example, there is a lengthy discussion of the meaning of once-born and twice-born (p.404) and several instances
of over-extended descriptions of the dangers entailed in "dealing with the Lord." All of this religious content is brought
forward again in the final moment of recognition. But it is too
weighty and too wordy to be carried by the action. Much of the
last few paragraphs consists of details and interpretations by
the author, rather than action and awareness centered specifically in the protagonist.

The *Violent Bear It Away* is clearly a description of the
Augustinian concept of grace. The world is good, but thoroughly
contaminated through the evil deeds of men and women. In this
redeemable world, which continues to exist after the grace-event,
there is a task to do. The prevailing evil must be unmasked (the
reversal of symbols); it must be defeated (the reversal of the
outcome of actions); and the reign of God must be recognized (the
moment of recognition).

The Third Variation: "The Lame Shall Enter First"

The third version of the initiation story, "The Lame Shall
Enter First," is, after "The Displaced Person," Flannery O'Connor's longest short story. In this "novella" she portrays a concept of grace significantly different from that depicted in either "The Artificial Nigger" or The *Violent Bear It Away*. As we
shall see, unlike its first version, this story is not Thomistic.
That is, grace does not enhance or ennoble human nature. The
symbols used in the novella are not multivalent in any way which
harmonizes the natural and supernatural orders. The discrepancy

in action between intention and outcome is not such that the
human intention is complemented to yield a result greater
than, but continuous with, that originally envisioned by the protagonist. The moment of recognition does not entail an understanding of a gift freely given by a beneficent source outside
of or beyond the control of the protagonist which contributes to
the maturation of the protagonist himself or herself.

Nor is the story Augustinian in its presentation of the actions of grace. Unlike the second variation, *The Violent Bear It
Away*, its symbols are not reversed in order to reveal goodness
amid the evil of human life. The discrepancy in action between
intention and outcome is not a reversal of the natural desire revealing a divine will which opposes and overrules natural intention. The moment of recognition is not one which reveals an order of meaning radically opposed to the apparent order of nature
and calls disordered nature to conversion.

The story is not Jansenistic in its portrayal of grace. Its
symbols do not undergo the displacement of their natural meanings
by supernatural meanings. Human actions are not stopped, nor do
intentions cease. There is a recognition on the part of the protagonist, unlike the merely secondary recognition in the Jansenistic stories. But the recognition is that within this life,
there is no grace. Matter and spirit are and remain irrevocably
opposed to one another.

It would seem at first glance that aspects of this third
variation, "The Lame Shall Enter First," are similar to our descriptions of Augustinian grace. However, a more exact and nu-
anced analysis will disclose that in fact there is no action of
grace in this story. There is only the revelation that nature and
supernature are diametrically opposed to one another in a dualistic understanding of reality. This opposition differs from that
found in the Augustinian stories, where there is also an opposing
relationship between the divine intention and sinful human desires, in that in this story the opposition is between two entirely separate realities: a world of light (spirit) and a world
of darkness (matter). Grace cannot penetrate the world of matter

to reveal its sinful condition and reverse it. There can be no reversal of intention from the natural to the supernatural except insofar as a character escapes altogether from the world of matter and darkness into the world of spirit and light.

Likewise, there is some similarity here to Jansenistic stories. One of the characters in "The Lame Shall Enter First," Norton, seems to be displaced, drawn gradually by the power of grace into a state discontinuous with his former self. In this he resembles Parker or Thomas' mother. Yet Norton is not displaced to be replaced by grace. He does not become a sign of divine power in the world, a sign of God's presence, because there is no presence of God in the world. God's power is elsewhere, completely separate from and alien to everything created. Norton is thus drawn out of the world of matter into the world of spirit. He is "displaced," but not in the Jansenistic sense. He is not replaced by grace, but removed altogether. In his place there is only darkness and emptiness.

For these reasons, "The Lame Shall Enter First" differs significantly from the three types of grace stories we have examined thus far. Whereas they depict various literary portrayals of the *presence* of grace, this story suggests rather the *absence* of grace. The context is still the question of the relationship of the natural and supernatural orders, and in this sense it can be called, as can all of O'Connor's stories, a "grace narrative." In this story, O'Connor has moved beyond her three most consistent depictions of grace (Thomistic, Augustinian and Jansenistic) to present a grace narrative which is analogous to Manichaeanism.[10] It is clear that O'Connor's presentations of grace range

---

[10] We are not interested here in a detailed history or description of Manichaeanism, either as originated by Manes (Mani, Manichaeus) in the third century A.D. or as developed by his later followers. Rather it is Manichaeanism's basic dualism which is of interest. This dualism is the basis both of cosmogeny and of soteriology in this religion (Ries, "Manichaeism," p. 156). In the beginning, before "creation," there were two entirely separate uncreated principles, Light and Darkness, two separate kingdoms ruled respectively by the Father of Greatness and the

over a spectrum of theological interpretations.

Use of Symbols

The use of symbols in "The Lame Shall Enter First" differs
significantly from that of the other three types of stories we
have examined, including the first two versions of this same literary theme, in that there is no multivalence. That is, in the
development of the narrative, the symbols are not single concepts
or images which change or reveal new meanings through reconciliation, reversal or displacement. Rather, in this story, we find
sets of dichotomous, unchanging symbols. In the place of one

Prince of Darkness (Ries, pp. 155-156). As a result of a war between them, some mixing of the two took place, and some Spirit
was imprisoned in Matter, some Light in Darkness, some Good in
Evil. For Manichaeanism redemption is accomplished by the gnos-
tic revelation of the eschatological re-separation of the two
kingdoms (Ries, pp. 155-156). Matter is not redeemed, since it
is irredeemable. Spirit will one day be removed again from Matter. This, together with strict asceticism which attempts, even
while the human Spirit is imprisoned in Matter, to avoid the material as much as possible by abstention from sex, meat, drink,
property, etc. (Ries, p. 156), constitutes the process of "redemption." Redemption is not by reconciliation, or by conversion, or even by replacement. Matter (Evil) is returned to the
realm of Darkness, while the Spirit (Good) escapes to the region
of Light.

　　We have noted some similarity in "The Lame Shall Enter
First" to Augustinian and Jansenistic narratives. It is interesting to note in this connection that Augustine was accused of
being a Manichaean when he pushed some of his opinions to extremes, emphasizing the corruption of nature in order to underline the need for the grace of conversion (Rondet, *Grace of
Christ*, pp. 107, 120). Though Augustine had been a Manichaean
for a time during his youth (*Confessions*, pp. 36-78), he cannot
be said to have held that teaching after his conversion to
Christianity. Indeed, he clearly claimed to reject Manichaean
dualism (*De nuptiis et concupiscentia*) II, 9). Nonetheless there
are elements in Augustinianism, and in Augustine himself, which
tend toward this extreme form of anti-matter dualism (see above,
pp. 34-37). Similarly, Jansenism shows clear affinity to Manichaeanism in its extreme emphasis on the corruption of human nature and in its ascetical piety which emphasizes a separation of
the spiritual and the sensible (see above, pp. 38-39; also
Matteucci, "Jansenistic Piety," pp. 825-826).

multivalent symbol, O'Connor employs sets of symbols whose meanings
are parallel opposites, reflecting the dualistic understanding of
reality which this story portrays.

A central set of symbols in the story are Rufus Johnson's
feet: one "lame" (physically deformed and unable to function
normally) and the other well-formed and "normal." Rufus' two
dissimilar feet symbolize the dual composition of existence.
His "normal" foot symbolizes natural, physical or material reality. The "lame" foot, though grotesque and abnormal on the natural level, symbolizes supernatural or spiritual reality. It
serves as a sacred object, a sign of divine election for Rufus.

Throughout the story, in a manner similar to the symbolic
meanings of his dissimilar feet, Rufus displays two separate sets
of personality attributes and world views. One aspect of his
character announces Jesus as the savior of humankind and functions to affirm and release the good spirit or light confined
within persons from its material condition back to the region of
Light. Jesus is here understood as the Lord of the Light. As
one of the elect himself (signified by the lame foot which is not
in conformity with the laws of nature), Rufus is a believer in
Jesus. Yet Rufus actively participates in Evil and claims to be
governed by Satan, the Prince of Darkness. The demonic aspects
of his life, including his destructive criminal behavior and his
ability to identify and confirm the evil within the social worker
who tries to reform his life, are symbolized by the normal (in
keeping with the rules of the matter) foot. As his feet retain
their dichotomous meanings throughout the narrative, so too does
he participate in a non-integrated way in the radical dualism of
human life, spirit (light) contained within the matter (darkness).

This paradoxical and dichotomous use of symbols is clarified
for the reader in a dialogue between Rufus, who is both a Bible-
quoting fundamentalist and a juvenile delinquent, and Sheppard,
who as an atheistic social worker tries to change the youth's
behavior patterns by an appeal to rational principles. Sheppard
suggests that Rufus' unacceptable destructive tendencies are

"compensation for the [lame] foot" (p. 450). He believes that
the boy will be able to correct his behavior once he understands
its roots. He further seeks to correct the essential problem by
having the lame foot fitted for an orthopedic shoe which will enable the boy to walk correctly and forget that this foot is abnormal. Rufus angrily protests, insisting that his evil deeds
have nothing to do with his crippled foot, but are caused by Satan who exercises power over him. He insists: "I lie and steal
because I'm good at it! My foot don't have a thing to do with
it! The lame shall enter first! The halt'll be gathered together. When I get ready to be saved, Jesus'll save me" (p. 480).

Rufus thus participates in the myths of both kingdoms, the
power of light and the power of darkness. Just as he possesses
an unnatural, spirit-defined foot, so too he reads the Bible and
preaches salvation by Jesus, yet his behavior is governed by Satan. Throughout the story, he recognizes and participates in aspects of both realms without himself experiencing the effects of
this dual-faceted life. Rufus is a static figure. He does not
undergo any change in the direction of good or evil. Through
him, however, the uselessness of Sheppard's secular priesthood
based on atheistic rationalism is confirmed as a product of the
material, dark world, while the spiritual goodness of Sheppard's
son Norton is released from the matter which confines it into the
Light. In neither case does the meaning of the symbol change.
The dichotomous nature of reality is merely acknowledged.

The symbol of lameness is also employed in the portrayal of
the other two characters in the story: Sheppard, the city recre-
ation director who spends his spare time trying to assist delinquent boys who show intellectual promise (which his own son Norton does not) to reform their lives, and Norton, his neglected
ten-year-old son. Sheppard is a spiritual cripple who fails to
recognize the evil in materialism. He refuses to acknowledge the
fundamental dualism within reality. He asserts that human persons can control their lives and shape their destinies through
the fuller use of their natural intellectual capacities. In Rufus he recognizes great intellectual prowess. Though he sees

Rufus as unfortunate because of his lame foot and his "warped" religious upbringing, he is persuaded that when Rufus understands his disabilities as the cause of his criminal activities, he will be able to overcome them and become a productive member of society. Ultimately, as he works with Rufus, trying to save him from the effects of his lame foot and his religious faith, Sheppard is outwitted by him. Sheppard's intellect is revealed as powerless to release Rufus from the darkness of matter in which he himself is hopelessly mired. The power of darkness continues to cripple Sheppard as he persists in his erroneous belief that humankind can save itself through its rational faculties. Sheppard's lameness, indicated at the outset of the story, is here demonstrated, not alleviated. At the close of the story, he remains in the darkness, bound to the earth.

Norton, who at the outset of the narrative is said to possess a "faded" light, is "lame" as a result of the restraint of his inner light by his overwhelming material existence. He is further debilitated by his father's attempt to sanctify matter and deny spiritual reality. As Norton struggles to be reunited with the light, his father denies its existence. Norton's mother (a figure of light, the opposite of his dark father) has died and Norton feels impelled to follow her. His father has told him that because she is now dead, his mother no longer exists. Rufus, however, befriends the boy, revealing to him continued life of the spirit beyond the confines of the body. This news, sparked by words of salvation read him from the Bible by Rufus, enkindles the light within Norton. Even Sheppard notices the presence of an "unnatural light" (p. 478) in Norton whom he has intellectually and psychologically abandoned due to the boy's low level of intelligence and his inability to forget his mother's death. As Rufus' presence reveals the darkness in Sheppard's life, so too he brings out the light within Norton. Finally, by the close of the story, Norton has found his mother as a light among the stars in the night sky. He ties up his body (symbolizing its uselessness or lameness), hanging himself in his father's dark attic. Freed of his material body, he escapes into the

light. Thus, in death, his spirit is freed from its bondage in
his material body and he becomes reunited with his mother in the
light.

A second set of symbols used in similar fashion to depict
the duality of light and darkness in the story are the dark attic
of Sheppard's house and the bright stars of the night sky. The
attic is without a source of light, except that reflected from
the night sky through the open window. O'Connor describes the
attic as a "jungle of shadows," barren rafters and packing
crates. There in the darkness, Sheppard has set up a telescope
through which he hopes to instruct Rufus on the unity of the universe and humankind's ability to conquer space.

Rufus has already discredited Sheppard's atheistic and rational approach to life's questions and he is uninterested in
physical nature. He tells Norton, "Don't waste your valuable
time, kid. You seen the moon once, you seen it" (p. 460). Norton, however, who has earlier been described to possess an inner
"faded light" which is characterized by one of his eyes which
does not focus well, but rather "lists" beyond the perimeters of
the immediate environment, and who is attracted by the light, begins using the telescope to search the night sky for his dead
mother.

At the close of the story, when he has been not only rejected, but repudiated by Rufus, Sheppard begins to see everything
in his life, including his own image, as shriveled and black. He
suddenly remembers Norton's empty and abandoned face. He rushes
to the child watching the stars in the attic. In his mind, he
sees Norton's face emblazoned with light. He thinks of this
child as the only possible source of light in his now blackened
existence. However, as he reaches the darkened attic, he sees
the child's abandoned body hanging in the shadows. Norton has
sought to leave his father's darkened house for the light promised by the image of his mother among the stars. Here again we
see that the dichotomy between the attic (material darkness) and
the night stars (spiritual light) is not in any way mediated or
changed. Sheppard is confirmed in the darkness of his attic,

while Norton is released from the material confines of his pater-
nal home to join his mother in the spiritual kingdom of light.

There are two sets of opposing symbols, each symbol signi-
fying only one of two dichotomous worlds: material darkness or
spiritual light. The two worlds remain apart from one another.
No "grace" can be given from the world of spirit which might redeem or in any way alter the world of matter. The two sets of
symbols are connected only by the telescope, which can suggest
the possibility of escape for Norton's spirit back to the region
of light where his mother dwells. This use of symbols is, therefore, quite different from the use of symbols found in stories
where O'Connor describes the presence of *active* grace. Here the
opposing and changeless sets of dichotomous symbols suggest the
absence of grace and the impossibility of any real redemption.

Discrepancy in Action

We have seen that Flannery O'Connor employs symbols in this
story in a way that is dualistic, employing sets of dichotomous
symbols in the place of single, multivalent ones. In a similar
way, O'Connor alters discrepancy in action for application to
"The Lame Shall Enter First." Because this story presents a different cosmology and therefore a different understanding of the
problem of grace, the device of discrepancy in action depicts
here not the presence of grace, but its absence. Due to the total dichotomy between the realms of spirit and matter in this
dualistic narrative, grace does not intervene in human actions.
Rather, actions which participate in the dichotomous separation
between these two realities achieve their respective goals as intended. However, human intentions which seek to eliminate or re-
concile these opposite principles are destined for failure because they pursue an impossible end.

Each of the three characters in the story acts. Norton, a
creature of the light, seeks and achieves spiritual liberation.
Rufus, a dual character who acknowledges the realm of the light
and on the basis of his belief in Jesus' saving power and his
own "sacred" foot, expects someday himself to be saved, but who

is dominated by darkness and governed in his actions by Satan, intends and accomplishes perverse and evil deeds. Sheppard sees himself as a good man who intends to eliminate evil through the use of created intelligence (material light). His actions fail because he attempts to redeem the irredeemable (matter), and to do so through a material instrument (spiritless, natural intelligence).

Norton is introduced into the narrative as a character who possesses an inner light. The light, however, is "faded" due to its embodiment in a dark, material world. The inner light, or spiritual dimension, does not influence Norton's human faculties or his moral behavior. Clearly this spiritual principle belongs to a realm other than his material existence. He is described as having only average or even low intelligence and various natural imperfections, including selfishness and greed. However, these are properties of his physical being. They do not influence his propensity toward spiritual light. As Norton becomes aware of the existence of the spiritual realm, his own inner light begins to burn more brightly. Whereas his relationship to his father, who seeks light in material reality, only increases the paralysis of Norton's own spirit, his relationship to Rufus, who, though he himself does not yet participate in the Kingdom of Light does know of its existence and is able to turn Norton in its direction, motivates him to seek the light ever more eagerly.

Using the telescope with which his father had intended to impress upon Rufus humankind's ability to conquer physical limitations through the use of innate intelligence (for example, his ability to travel in space and eventually to control his cosmic destiny), Norton searches the heavens for his dead mother whom he believes to dwell in the Kingdom of Light. As Norton continues his quest for the light, he gradually divests himself of his dark, material connections, including his relationship with his father. His search ends when Norton believes he has found his mother in the night sky among the stars. He asserts complete confidence in the dawning light, calling out to his father, "I've found her! Mama! Come and look!" (p. 478). Though his father dismisses his claim as merely starlight, Norton acts to unite himself with the light he has found. From the attic rafters, above the telescope and facing the window into the starlight, Norton hangs himself. In this final act, he accomplishes his intention to escape the darkness of his earthly existence with Sheppard into the realm of light or spirit represented by his mother. There is no discrepancy in his action. It is the fitting conclusion to the struggle to free the inner light, formerly faded and trapped in the darkness of his material existence.

Sheppard, the story's protagonist, has two original intentions. His primary intention is to save Rufus Johnson from a life of criminal activity and destructive behavior. He wishes to initiate him into society by appealing to his natural intellectual ability and by correcting his lameness. Sheppard's secondary intention is to teach his son, Norton, to share his material possessions with others. Sheppard fails to accomplish either intention: demanding natural virtue from Norton, he does not see the child's developing inner light; refusing to acknowledge the power of evil in matter, he tries to reform Rufus through natural, material rationality. In seeking to establish a single "good" universe regulated through the power of the human mind and technological skill, Sheppard violates the basic dualistic nature of reality. He is ultimately shown to be powerless to alter the dichotomous worlds of matter (darkness) and spirit (light). At the conclusion of the story, Rufus has been returned to jail to face new charges of breaking and entering and robbery, and Norton has committed suicide, which from Sheppard's natural point of view is the ultimately selfish act. Sheppard is left alone to face the consequences of his naive understanding of the nature of reality and his own impotent actions.

Rufus Johnson is presented as a dualistic character throughout the story. He both believes in the saving power of Jesus, the Lord of Light, and knows himself to be possessed by Satan, the prince of Darkness. Since Rufus recognizes the existence of these two separate realms, he is able to function to some extent in each. That is, his actions are properly ordered to maintain the underlying dualism to which he is a witness.

Rufus intends to destroy the self-proclaimed secular messiah, Sheppard, through a series of predatory acts. To this end, he accepts Sheppard's invitation to share his home with himself and his son. Rufus outwits Sheppard and discredits his position as a professional social worker by using the protection of Sheppard's home and friendship with his innocent son as alibis for his continuing crimes. His final victory over Sheppard comes through his part in Norton's suicide. In large part to spite Sheppard, Rufus encourages Norton's pursuit of the boy's dead mother. When Norton hangs himself to rejoin her in heaven, Rufus scores his final victory over the child's father. In relation to its significance for Sheppard, who seeks salvation within the natural realm, Rufus' encouragement of death is the culminating act of perversity and destruction. In direct contradiction to Sheppard's denial of the existence of evil and his intention to establish the kingdom of light within the order of human nature, Rufus has acted to bring Sheppard to the brink of the pit (the darkness of hell). Thus Rufus' intention is successfully accomplished. He has revealed to the would-be secular savior the overwhelming power of evil and has taken away from him his only real light, his own son Norton.

When Rufus befriends Norton, his primary motivation is his hatred of Sheppard. However, he does lead Norton toward the light which the child seeks. Rufus instructs Norton concerning the Kingdom of Jesus from a bible which he has stolen for this purpose. Though Norton had watched Rufus commit the theft, Rufus did not permit him to participate in the crime lest the innocent child be corrupted. Though he himself is ruled by the power of darkness, Rufus believes in Jesus and is thus able to recognize the spiritual goodness and light within Norton which Sheppard denies. He is able to aid Norton and to lead him toward the light, but he himself does not yet live in the spirit. For this reason, Rufus neither fully comprehends the light which Norton experiences nor does he accompany Norton on his final, liberating journey into the light. Though Rufus believes that he is ultimately predestined to heaven, he knows that his salvation is not yet accomplished. Remaining under the power of Satan, he continues intending and performing evil acts, expecting that at some later time, he too, like Norton, will be brought forth into the Kingdom of Light. In the meantime, he continues his dual life, knowing of the existence of the light, but participating in the dark, evil aspects of life.

The key to understanding the relationship between action and intention in this story is the maintenance of the duality in reality. Actions performed within each realm properly motivated with regard to the order which contains them are successfully accomplished because of their essential appropriateness. However, actions which ignore or seek to eliminate the dichotomy between good and evil, spirit and matter, are failures because of their impossibility in a dualistic universe.

Moment of Recognition

In the moment of recognition, the dichotomous meanings of the symbol sets are affirmed and the appropriateness of actions is revealed. The recognition here is not that of a maturation, conversion or replacement brought about through the operation of grace, but a confirmation of the irresolvable dichotomy between the two realms of Jesus and Satan. The first realm is characterized by light, goodness and spirit; the second by darkness, evil and matter. The moment of recognition differs then from that found in stories previously discussed in that what is acknowledged is not an intervention of the divine which has brought about some change in the human condition, but rather the revelation of a dualistic, unchangeable universe.

Because he participates from the beginning of the story in both the realms of Jesus and Satan (though not in any integrating or dynamic way), Rufus Johnson cannot in any true sense be said to experience a moment of recognition at the outcome of the story. At the conclusion of the narrative, he is being returned to the jail from which he had been briefly released. However, his condition is in no way altered by the development of the

plot. Rather, through his presence, Norton has been released
from the darkness into the light and his father has been brought
to some understanding of his place in the dualistic cosmic order.
Rufus, then, serves essentially as a catalyst for action and
meaning concerning the lives of others in the story.

For other reasons, Norton cannot be said to participate in
the moment of recognition in the usual meaning of the term.
Though we have been told that he sees his mother in the light of
the night sky and that he has shed his material body to join her
in the heavens, this light within Norton which escapes matter to
become part of the Kingdom of Light can hardly be said to represent the character, Norton, moving on into spiritual liberation.
Rather, all that has been described as Norton, including his intellect, will, body and all his human attributes, are shed in
this passage into the light. The inner "unnatural" light has
been freed, but its freedom is accomplished at the total cost of
the person of Norton.

The only character who can be said to experience recognition
within the narrative is Sheppard. From the outset unable to accept the evidence for the existence of the two irreconcilable
kingdoms, he has tried to establish his own order of a unified,
good nature through the use of human (material) will power and
intellection. However, he has failed due to the impossibility of
redeeming matter by material, natural means. At the close of the
story, Sheppard is forced to acknowledge the existence of evil
and to rush toward the light which he has earlier seen, but ignored in Norton. However, Norton's light is not an earthly
light. He has already moved beyond the physical realm, leaving
Sheppard alone in the overwhelming darkness.

At the beginning of the narrative, Sheppard has already
judged Norton to be hopeless on the basis of his natural virtues
and vices. Casting Norton aside, Sheppard chooses to work with
Rufus, who demonstrates a higher intellectual capacity and presents a greater challenge because of his criminal record and his
unfortunate history and physical condition. Throughout the
course of events, though Rufus rejects Sheppard's attempts to

help him, including the purchase of a special shoe designed to normalize his walking ability, a telescope and a microscope, Sheppard clings determinedly to the belief that he will save the boy from his evil ways.

As Rufus' destructive behavior and hatred of Sheppard become more manifest, Norton begins increasingly to reveal an inner light. Sheppard notices the unnatural light, but deliberately ignores its presence in order to give his undivided attention to enkindling the natural light within Rufus. Believing himself to be a light which "ravages Rufus, hitting dead center" (p. 451), Sheppard carefully focuses his attention on Rufus waiting for some evidence of a "memory of the lost light" (p. 452). When Norton finally calls out to Sheppard that he has found the light of his dead mother in the starry sky, Sheppard reproves him for this nonsense and sends the child to bed. At another point, when Norton beckons Sheppard to speak to him of one of Rufus' crimes, Sheppard hesitates, looks toward the light emanating from Norton, acts as if he sees nothing and passes on beyond the child's doorway.

Sheppard's concentration on Rufus, however, proves to be in vain. Rufus reveals to him that he has used Sheppard to cover for his continuing criminal activity. After an argument concerning how Rufus' salvation might be accomplished (Rufus reiterating his position that only Jesus can save him from the power of Satan and Sheppard denying the existence of Satan and asserting that he himself has the ability to save Rufus if he will only cooperate), Rufus shouts that the Devil has Sheppard in his power and departs from Sheppard's home. Later that evening, police sirens pierce the night. The police bring Rufus to the door. Rufus tells the police that they have only captured them because he wanted to teach Sheppard a lesson. Rufus then accuses Sheppard of making immoral suggestions (regarding questions of heaven and hell) to him. Sheppard immediately denies the allegations to the police and justifies himself to them. He tells them: "He knows that's not true. He knows he's lying. I did everything I knew how for him. I did more for him than I did for my own child. I hoped to

save him and I failed, but it was an honorable failure. I have
nothing to reproach myself with" (p. 480).

As the police take Rufus away, he calls out: "The lame'll
carry off the prey!" (p.481). Rufus's voice is jubilant. Sheppard moves quickly from a feeling of self-justification to one of
panic. He realizes that he has virtually ignored Norton all this
time. Rufus' words ring as a threat in his mind. He sees Rufus
as a "clear-eyed-Devil" (p. 481). In panic he rushes to Norton
in the attic by the telescope, but it is too late. Rufus' threat
has come true. Norton has been carried off as prey by the destructive suggestions of Rufus. Sheppard finds the dead child's
body hanging in the darkened attic. His own savior image, previously undermined by Rufus, and briefly transferred to Norton as
the bearer of the light, disappears completely as Sheppard's
world blackens. All hope of salvation is gone.

Sheppard recognizes all too fully his terrible error. In
this final scene, Rufus has been revealed to him as a true demon
who has tested him and proved him to be false and worthless. He
has further taken from him the only light which existed for Sheppard. Norton, his own son who could have provided light for his
life, earlier ignored and cast aside, is no longer present.
Sheppard faces the dualistic reality which he has sought to deny.
He stands as a man condemned by his own pride and blindness,
overwhelmed in the darkness.

* * *

"The Lame Shall Enter First" depicts a world in which no
grace can intervene to alter the separate orders of matter and
spirit. The symbols used in the narrative are dichotomous, referring respectively to the two divergent realms. Natural human
intentions to unite these realms or to redeem matter are rejected
as impossible, whereas those intentions to maintain the separation of grace or to reveal it to the ignorant are accomplished.
The working of grace is not involved in either process. In the
moment of recognition the protagonist becomes aware of the dichotomous realities of matter and spirit and of the impossibility

of his materialistic humanism.　The third variation is thus a
new type of grace narrative, a story which in its insistence on
cosmic dualism suggests analogy to Manichaean theology.

CHAPTER FOUR
TWO LIMIT STORIES: THE EXPANSION OF THE SPECTRUM

The two prior chapters examined divers types of grace narratives. By analyzing Flannery O'Connor's use of key literary devices, we discovered three different approaches to the operation of grace in her fiction. In the final section of Chapter Three we found that in addition to these three more common types, O'Connor also created a type of grace narrative differing significantly from them. "The Lame Shall Enter First," though in some respects resembling Augustinian and Jansenistic stories, uses the literary devices in such a way as to present a new mode, analogous to a Manichaean understanding of the relation of nature and supernature. According to this approach, no grace can be given to material nature, since it is irredeemably separated from the realm of Spirit and Light.

Our examination of this story, then, has prompted the extension of our analytical model. There are not merely three types of grace narratives presented in Flannery O'Connor's fiction, but (at least) four. Yet this fourth type is not really a type of *grace* at all. It is better described as a depiction of a dualistic cosmos in which grace cannot be given. It can be included as a type of "grace narration" only in the sense that it is written, as are all O'Connor stories, in the larger context of the relationship of the supernatural and the natural (we have seen that O'Connor considered *all* her fiction to be generally concerned with the "action of grace").[1] But, in "The Lame Shall Enter First" there is no divine intervention in nature. This Manichaean narrative portrays a universe devoid of redemptive grace.

---

[1]*Mystery and Manners*, p. 118 (see above, pp. 21-22).

Two further exceptions appear in O'Connor's fiction. Like "The Lame Shall Enter First," the two limit stories extend our analytical model and present approaches to the relationship of nature and supernature which suggest the absence of grace.

One of these stories is a narrative of "no grace." "The Partridge Festival" is nihilistic. This story portrays the need for grace, and insists on the potential for grace, but no grace is given. No meaning is given to the meaninglessness of the natural order, though the need for such meaning is apparent. Here there is no use of multivalent symbols, no discrepancy in action, and the recognition is that of "no grace." In a sense, this story is at one pole of the grace spectrum. It goes beyond even the Manichaean narrative in which, though nature remains unredeemed, redemption takes place in the liberation of the spirit or light from the darkness of matter. Here even escape is impossible; if the supernatural level exists at all, it chooses not to be involved in any way with the natural.

The other story is a narrative of "all grace." "Judgement Day" portrays nature to be so closely related to grace that no distinction between the two is possible. There is no use of multivalent symbols, no discrepancy in action, and a recognition that human actions possess the capacity to fulfill their own intentions with no further need for grace. This story is analogous to Pelagianism, in that there is no supernatural quality to grace. Persons do not need divine grace for salvation. They can save themselves by their own freely chosen acts. This narrative is at the opposite pole of the grace spectrum to "The Partridge Festival."

It is interesting to note that these two stories were both considered by O'Connor for inclusion in her short story collection, *Everything That Rises Must Converge*.[2] O'Connor at first

---

[2]For a brief description of this matter in letters to her literary agent and her publisher, see *Habit of Being*, pp. 575, 579-580, 589.

submitted "The Partridge Festival," but later claimed that this
"farce" was "just not up to the others."[3]   What makes this decision so interesting is that "The Partridge Festival" is the only work in O'Connor's corpus in which there is a clearly developed nihilistic depiction. Whereas other stories reveal pessimism concerning the possibility of salvation, "The Partridge Festival" is the only O'Connor narrative which portrays a world
where grace is not only needed, but anticipated, yet not received.
O'Connor published the story separately, as she did most of her
other short stories. However, she withdrew it from inclusion in
the second collection.

It is impossible to know for certain her motivation in making the substitution. But it is interesting to note that the
replacement story, "Judgement Day," presents the opposite view of
grace. From a portrayal of a world where divine intervention is
needed and sought, but not received, O'Connor turns to a depiction of a world in which grace as such is not needed. Human nature itself is sufficient for salvation, and human persons can
avail themselves of this "natural grace." "Judgement Day" is not
only at the opposite end of the grace spectrum from the nihilistic "Partridge Festival," but it is also more optimistic than any
of Flannery O'Connor's other stories. Examined from the perspective of the operation of supernatural grace, however, both of
these stories are similar in that both depict grace more by its
absence than its presence. "The Partridge Festival" refuses to
offer the grace needed by human nature and "Judgement Day" considers human nature to be its own natural grace. In the former
story the protagonist asks for grace and finds none; in the latter work the protagonist needs no grace to achieve his goals.

It cannot be argued that by this substitution O'Connor made
any definitive decision regarding her most successful depictions
of grace and nature or a theological option among the many types
of grace portrayed during her literary career. But it does seem

---

[3]*Habit of Being*, pp. 432, 579.

clear that in making the final selection for inclusion in what
she knew to be her last major published work, she preferred to
conclude her artistic career with the more optimistic "Judgement
Day" than with the nihilistic view portrayed in "The Partridge
Festival."

"The Partridge Festival"

"The Partridge Festival" depicts a world in which grace is
desired, even expected, but not received. Because this narrative
presents a "no grace" situation, O'Connor employs the literary
devices differently from their applications in other stories
which present the actions of grace. Unlike the symbols in Thomistic, Augustinian and Jansenistic works, the symbols in "The
Partridge Festival" do not change to ennoble, reverse or replace
the naturally suggested meanings. Nor do they reveal the dual-
ities of good and evil within reality as the sets of symbols do
in the Manichaean story. Rather the symbols here are flat, that
is, thoroughly naturalistic. There is no composite meaning, reversal or replacement to indicate the active presence of any level of meaning or order of reality other than the apparent, literal one.

There is in "The Partridge Festival" no discrepancy in action between intention and outcome effected by an intervening divine will or even conflicting supernatural powers. Rather the
characters here obtain a result that is consistent with their actions. They reap what they have sown. In fact, O'Connor emphasizes this point in the story by having her characters "expect"
something more than they deserve--some intrusion of grace or
good fortune--into their hopelessly banal situation. But they
receive no grace, no change of fortune. There is no discrepancy
between their intentions and the outcomes of their actions.

In this narrative, there is no true moment of recognition,
no sense of gift, no call to conversion, no Christ-sign. Rather
these characters conclude their actions in an attitude of despair.
In their world, there is no surprise to acknowledge. There are
no ennobling, reversing or replacing events. They look for and

expect a Savior, but find none. The story is nihilistic.[4]

The key symbol in this story is the azalea, a flower which grows in profusion in the town of Partridge, the ancestral home of the protagonist, a salesman turned writer named Calhoun. The flower is used on badges to promote the town's annual festival. Calhoun's great-grandfather initiated the Azalea Festival and coined its motto: "Beauty is Our Money Crop" (p. 426). To Calhoun, the azalea represents both natural beauty reduced to mere commodity and his own lineage in a family dominated by commercialism. Though he does not yet experience an enthusiasm like his great-grandfather's toward the Azalea Festival, he is sensitive to the power of materialism represented by the azalea. He views the azalea as lethal because he knows that he is infected with the drive toward salesmanship:

> In the face of a customer, he was carried outside himself; his face began to beam and sweat and all complexity left him; he was in the grip of a drive as strong as the drive of some men for liquor or a woman; and he was horribly good at it. He was so good at it that the company had given him an achievement scroll (p. 425).

Though knowing himself to be a master salesman, Calhoun hopes to discover some way to overcome this rampant drive toward materialism in order to become a writer, artist or mystic. In order to accomplish this, he seeks to replace the deadly azalea with a saving symbol in what is his first attempt to move from sales to artistic creation.

For his first story as an aspiring writer, Calhoun turns his attention from the azalea to a suffering rebel who like himself

---

[4]By "nihilistic" is meant not any particular anarchistic or revolutionary movement--the nineteenth century Russian literary and political usage of the term is often specified as "Nihilism"--but rather the general contemporary usage of the term as denoting an attitude that negates any ultimate meaning on which a coherent and defensible moral and religious order might be built. Ultimate truth, value, societal coherence, even being itself are shown to be nothing or to tend toward nothingness (see "Nihilism," *Encyclopaedia Britannica*; and Lotz, "Nihilismus," pp. 963-965). Atheistic existentialism is one of the most important modern expressions of this philosophy (Lotz, pp. 963-965).

has refused to participate in the promulgation of the azalea. This man, Singleton, refused to purchase the required azalea badge to be worn during the festival. Since this "offense" Singleton has been driven mad by the angry townspeople. He becomes in Calhoun's mind the image of the innocent victim whose suffering expiates Calhoun's own materialism.

However, in the outcome of the story, Singleton is revealed not to be a grace-filled or saving figure. He is merely a madman who has no power. Though Calhoun has tried to think of the man as his spiritual kin who will free him from his own propensity toward superficiality and the profit-incentive, Singleton is not an adequate replacement symbol. The azalea retains its powerful position as the central symbol in the tale.

The meaning of the azalea is not replaced or altered. Its significance for Calhoun remains. The festival continues, the azaleas flourish and Calhoun realizes that he will not be saved. He, too, is tainted by the azalea. As a master salesman after the tradition of his great-grandfather, he will spend his life promoting and profiting from unending azalea festivals.

Both Calhoun and a young woman named Mary Elizabeth are former residents of Partridge who have returned to the town intending to write accounts of the sensational event which has occured at the opening of the Azalea Festival. Calhoun and Mary Elizabeth have heard the news of how a man named Singleton shot six people to death on the opening day of the festival. Though townspeople have judged the man insane and committed him to the local mental hospital, the two neophyte writers, each on an initial and self-imposed assignment, intend to research and record the true facts of the case.

Mary Elizabeth and Calhoun hope to prove that Singleton was an innocent outsider who maintained himself at the fringe of this society, an independent thinker who refused to lower himself to the level of the townspeople, a Christ-type who is being crucified by local residents who themselves bear the real guilt for the murders. The two young writers have learned that Singleton refused to purchase a required Azalea Festival badge. For this, he was imprisoned in public stocks, tried by a mock court and finally jailed with a goat previously convicted for the same offense. Upon his release, Singleton had shot five of the town's dignitaries and an innocent by-stander. The murderer was immediately captured and committed without a trial to Quincy State Mental Hospital.

Townspeople whom Calhoun interviews feel vindicated that Singleton is confined at Quincy, the proper place for a crazy man. However, both Calhoun and Mary Elizabeth condemn the town for burying its dead so quickly, for continuing the festival without serious interruption even to mourn its lost citizens, and for now beginning to profit by the increased attention called to the festival by the tragedy. They view Singleton as a Christ-type who has brought divine judgment upon the town for its materialistic values, but who has been rejected by these hard-hearted people. They hope to vindicate this innocent man who has been condemned by a faithless, unrepentant society.

In order to meet their hero and offer him their loyal support, they visit the mental hospital. Stating that they are Singleton's relatives (and believing themselves to be his "spiritual" kin), they are granted a brief visit with Singleton. Though they accomplish their intention to meet him and gather sufficient data for their written accounts, the additional revelation does not happen. Whereas they had expected a Christ-figure, a god to save this disbelieving society, they discover that the man is, indeed, insane. While Calhoun tries to explain their empathy for his position, Singleton begins to make suggestive remarks to Mary Elizabeth and exposes himself to her. The hoped-for savior reveals himself not to be divine, but all man. There is no salvation, no hope.

Here there is not discrepancy in action, even though Calhoun and Mary Elizabeth expect the intervention of grace. They have come to see a madman, and they have seen him. They sought the facts in the case, in order to record them. They have accomplished this end. Their further hope that they might find in Singleton a savior remains unrealized. They had desired more than they deserved, salvation from themselves and their own lives. However, they receive only what can be naturally expected. They enter the company of a deranged man. He offers only self-exposure, nothing more. The discrepancy wished for and anticipated fails to happen.

In keeping with the hopeless, natural condition of humankind which the narrative depicts, the recognition is only that of an unredemptive event. Calhoun and Mary Elizabeth are forced by Singleton's "epiphany" to acknowledge that there is no grace. Singleton is indeed crazy and irresponsible. His action has had no meaning in the order of salvation. Their view that he is a suffering victim, a Christ sacrificed by society, is unfounded. He is not an agent of change, a bearer of truth, or an expiator for the sins of society. Indeed, here there is no savior. The situation remains what it is, unredeemed. Singleton's true story is already known. Calhoun may retell it, but he remains a salesman. The story is a nihilistic narrative.

"Judgement Day"

The world portrayed in "Judgement Day" is one in which the action of grace is neither desired nor experienced. There is here no distinction between nature and supernature. For this reason, there is a sense in which the story can be considered as "all grace." The story is the account of a man's ability to participate knowingly and confidently in his own salvation. At the outset of the tale, the protagonist judges himself to be an alien, exiled from his true home. He gradually recognizes what he must do to change this condition and reestablish his life in its proper order and place. He then methodically takes the necessary steps to obtain his salvation, confident that whatever assistance he requires will be available.

In this narrative, the symbols are not multivalent. Rather, the two orders of the natural and the supernatural are collapsed into one single "naturally graced" meaning. This meaning does not change as the plot develops. Nor is there any discrepancy in action. The goal sought by the protagonist is accomplished.

The recognition takes place throughout the early part of the story when the protagonist becomes aware of his uprooted condition and realizes that he can effect the change required to return to his true "home."

Because there are no multivalent symbols and no discrepancy in action, and because the moment of recognition is not an awareness of supernatural intervention in the course of human events, we can say that this narrative depicts more the absence of grace than the active presence of grace. Though in this it is similar to "The Lame Shall Enter First" and "The Partridge Festival," this story is neither Manichaean nor nihilist. Unlike "The Lame Shall Enter First," there are no sets of dichotomous symbols existing in a dualistic cosmos. In this story there is no dichotomy of meaning or action. Unlike "The Partridge Festival," there is not the recognition of "no grace," but rather an abiding awareness of "all grace." Since this story suggests that human action possesses the capacity to fulfill its own intention without the intervention of supernatural grace, it presents a new mode analogous to a Pelagian understanding of nature and grace.[5]

---

[5]Like the other theological schools we have described as bearing some resemblance to O'Connor's different types of grace, "Pelagianism" as we refer to it is not limited to the direct opinions of its founder. Indeed, it is controversial whether or not Pelagius himself ever developed systematically his approach to grace and nature (see, for example, Brown, *Augustine of Hippo*, p. 345, who argues that the Pelagian system was more Augustine's than Pelagius'--that Augustine systematized it in order to refute it; and McKenna, "Pelagius," p. 58, who states that the doctrine can be reconstructed from the known writings of Pelagius). "Pelagianism" refers generally to an approach to the relationship of nature and grace according to which grace is merely natural, an external help readily available to human persons. Salvation, or at least the first steps leading to it--this latter point separates Semi-Pelagian from the original Pelagian doctrine--can be merited by the human person (Rondet, *Grace of Christ*, pp. 112-116; McKenna, "Pelagius," p. 58; McKenna, "Semi-Pelagianism," p. 75). Original sin does not incapacitate human freedom, and persons thus remain capable on their own of choosing the good (Rondet, pp. 108-110; McKenna, "Pelagius," p. 58). According to Pelagianism, grace is merely something natural and something external. It is the power of the human will to choose the good, and it is the helps given externally by the Law of the Scriptures and

The key symbol in the story is "home." Tanner, the protagonist, is an elderly Southerner who has been uprooted from his
primitive Georgian home to live in a middle class New York apartment with his daughter. Though he now resides with her family in
respectable circumstances, he yearns to return home. For him,
his new life in the North is hell. He is completely alienated by
the urban environment of the city, the loss of his black friend
Coleman and his dependency on his daughter.

Home for Tanner is the South. It is his natural dwelling
place and his final destiny. He is unable to distinguish between the life he shared with Coleman in their shack near Corinth, Georgia, and the promise of eternal life. For him they are
one and the same. When he begins to realize that he is losing
his physical strength and may die in the North, Tanner becomes
eager to return quickly to his own home. He fears the possibility that his daughter, despite her promises to the contrary,
would bury him in the North should he die in New York. This
would mean the eternal loss of "home." He must return to the
South in order to save himself from this terrible destiny.

At the outcome of the story, Tanner is dead, but he has
been brought back to Georgia. He has died confident that he will
reach home; whether dead or alive is inconsequential to him.
Though he actually dies in New York and is briefly buried there,
his body is exhumed in keeping with his desire and he is finally
buried in the South. The single meaning of the symbol is retained. He has returned home. In death, as in life, the South

---

by the example of Christ (Rondet, pp. 112-117; McKenna, "Pelagius," p. 58; O'Grady, *Christian Anthropology*, pp. 78-79). The
necessity of the grace of Christ as an internal principle without
which the person cannot attain salvation or perform truly good
actions is thus denied, since the person is not essentially disordered by concupiscence. Though "Pelagianism" stands at the
other end of the grace spectrum from "Jansenism," "Manichaeanism"
and "nihilism" from this perspective of the person's natural
goodness, it is interesting to note that Pelagius demanded extreme asceticism if one were to merit salvation (Rondet, pp. 108-
112; Brown, pp. 342-348). In this aspect Pelagianism resembles
Jansenism and Manichaeanism.

is his true home.

There is no discrepancy in action between intention and outcome in this story. The protagonist is able correctly to assess
his dilemma and he is equally capable of acting to resolve it.
Other characters and elements in the tale participate as external factors which co-operate to carry the intention forward, con-
firming the underlying world view that all things work together
naturally toward the achievement of human goals.

Tanner's intention is to return to his native home in Georgia. He does not expect to live through this final trip, but
his own physical survival is not his concern. "It was the being
there that mattered; the dead or alive did not" (p. 532). His
stress is merely on getting home. How this is accomplished is
immaterial to him. He does know that he must initiate his journey and take what precautions he can against failure. However,
he is confident that should his own strength fail him he will be
aided enroute and will achieve his goal.

Tanner's certitude is based on his understanding of judgment. He tells his daughter that on Judgement Day "The sheep'll
be separated from the goats. Them that kept their promises from
them that didn't. Them that did the best they could with what
they had from them that didn't" (p. 541). This statement is the
key to his action and to his understanding of it. He intends to
use fully his limited strength to expedite his own safe return
home. On the merit of his good intention, he expects to achieve
his intended result. Having judged himself, he is confident of
the positive judgment of the Lord. For Tanner, these two judgments are one. However, he has less confidence in his daughter.
Though she had earlier promised to ship his body back to the
South should he die while living with her, she now shows signs of
breaking her promise. Unable to rely on her full participation
in the final course of events, Tanner reassumes control of his
destiny.

On the day before he intends to begin his journey home, he
carefully writes out instructions concerning his burial and the
disposition of his goods for his trusted friend Coleman. He pins

these inside his shirt pocket to prevent them from being lost
should he die before he reaches his destination. The note,
which also warns Coleman against coming North himself, includes
the specific directive: "If found dead ship express to Coleman
Parrum, Corinth, Georgia" (p. 531).

Upon discovering how much strength he has had to expend to
write the note, Tanner spends the remainder of the day recuper-
ating. On the day of his departure, he allows his daughter to
dress him, thus saving his own energy for the trip. Once the
daughter leaves the apartment to do some shopping, he sets out
secretly himself.

> All he had to do was push one foot in front of the other
> until he got to the door and down the steps. Once down
> the steps, he would get out of the neighborhood. Once
> out of it, he would hail a taxi cab and go to the freight
> yards. Some bum would help him onto a car. Once he got
> in the freight car, he would lie down and rest. During
> the night the train would start South, and the next day
> or the morning after, dead or alive he would be home (pp.
> 531-532).

He leaves the apartment, but he is barely able to reach the top
of the stairs. He stumbles and falls. He is found in the stair-
well by a hostile black man whom he at first believes to be his
friend Coleman. The man forces Tanner's dying body between the
stairposts in a kind of mock crucifixion position. Unwittingly,
the black man enables Tanner to continue his journey, for Tanner
dies there. His body is discovered by his daughter who temporarily buries it in New York, but finally fulfills her earlier
promise and has the body exhumed for proper burial, as Tanner
intended, back home in Georgia.

The unfolding of human events in such a way that the protagonist's original intention is accomplished depicts an "all grace"
narrative. That is, there is no discrepancy in this narrative
because the human and divine wills are the same. Tanner has intended to return finally to the South. He has from the outset
of the story believed this natural intention to be in keeping
with the supernatural intention. His death and the somewhat de-
layed return of his body are dismissed as irrelevant to the meaning of the story. The essential point is that he has known what

he must do and has proceeded to carry out his action to the best of his ability. This is all that is required to obtain salvation. The details are attended to through the external complementary acts of others who, as in the case of the black man, may not understand the meaning of their own actions in this regard.

The mock crucifixion scene is of note. O'Connor has depicted the event in such a way as to indicate that the black man is not guilty of Tanner's death. When Tanner calls out to him as a friend to help him, the man co-operates in a way he does not realize. Acting as an external aid toward the intended goal, the black man has expedited Tanner's progress toward his home.

Further, Tanner's death is not portrayed as redemptive or expiatory. The story is not moral in its intent. None of the story's characters have been condemned and thus none need to be saved. Tanner is merely making his way home. The manner of his approach to his final destination is according to the example of Christ's own death. Christ here seems only to serve as a model.

The recognition in the story takes place gradually as the protagonist comes to realize that although he is presently in an alienated state, away from his home, he will be able through the use of his own natural capacities to return to the place where he truly belongs. He becomes further aware that his goal to return home is in keeping with both his own capacity and the divine intention. For these reasons, he does not require or expect a supernatural intervention. Rather, he recognizes that since there is no difference in significance or intention between the supernatural and the natural, he does naturally participate in "grace." There is no requirement for intervention by the divine. Tanner does himself participate in the order of salvation and by that awareness, he is able to both judge and save himself.

Because there is no multivalent symbol, no discrepancy in action and the positive recognition that nature is one with supernature, the story is a Pelagian grace narrative. Here grace is indistinguishable from human meanings and intentions, and the recognition is a positive or optimistic one based on the understanding that human nature is sufficient for salvation. For this

reason, there is no action or operation of supernatural grace in
the narrative.

* * *

With "Judgement Day," our study of the types of grace narratives in Flannery O'Connor's fiction is complete. There is a
range of such types, including both stories which depict the
presence of grace and those which suggest the absence of grace.

O'Connor's six different types of grace narratives can be
summarized as follows:

Stories	Multivalence	Discrepancy	Recognition
Thomistic	harmony	continuity	maturation
Augustinian	opposition	reversal	call to conversion
Jansenistic	displacement	cessation	none (secondary)
Manichaean	none (dichotomous sets)	dualism	revelation of dualism
Nihilistic	none (nihilism)	none (static)	pessimism
Pelagian	none (naturalism)	none (dynamic)	optimism

* * *

The purpose of this study has been to describe and to analyze the ways in which Flannery O'Connor creates stories which
have as their central focus the operation of divine grace in the
world of women and men. We have discovered that her portrayals
of the action of grace as "totally believable yet totally unexpected" range across a wide spectrum of types, utilizing literary devices in various ways and resulting in types of grace narratives which are analogous to divergent theological approaches
to the relationship of divine grace to human nature. We have
shown, contrary to the opinion of many scholars, that O'Connor

cannot be said to limit her literary depiction of grace to one or even a few similar theological schools. Her literary creations include approaches to grace which are in fact strikingly different and which include, but move beyond, the boundaries of orthodoxy.

Our method of analysis has been to study the literary structure of her stories, to describe how the very process by which O'Connor conceives and develops her narratives determines the type of grace characteristic of each work. To do this we have discussed three literary devices which are essential to an analysis of her stories, whose central focus is the action of grace. By a detailed study of the precise modes in which O'Connor uses the devices of multivalent symbols, discrepancy in action between intention and outcome, and moment of recognition, we have been able to distinguish the various types of grace which she depicts. We have shown that this kind of analysis moves beyond studies limited to examination of external "religious" elements in the plot or of "religious" conceptual content. It is precisely this method which has enabled us to demonstrate that there is not a single theology of grace in O'Connor's fiction, but many.

We have discovered three types of grace narrations which portray the active presence of God's grace in human lives. These three types of stories, Thomistic, Augustinian and Jansenistic, are distinguished from one another by the various ways in which O'Connor uses the literary devices. We have also discovered, however, that in a few of her stories O'Connor creates literary representations of the absence of active grace. Her concern in these stories remains the relationship of God and the world, the question of ultimate meaning of human life in a theological context. Through an altered use of the literary devices, O'Connor depicts this absence of grace which neither changes nor saves nature.

In her fiction, then, Flannery O'Connor, when confronting the theological paradox which lies at the heart of the Christian tradition concerning creation and redemption, nature and grace, sin and salvation, freedom and predestination, explicates the

full range of ways in which God may be said to work in human history. Perhaps it is this studied exploration of possibilities
within the human-divine context that causes Flannery O'Connor's
fiction to continue to command the attention of the theologian of
literature as well the common reader.

APPENDIX

CHRONOLOGY OF THE LIFE AND WORKS

OF FLANNERY O'CONNOR

In addition to the significant events in the life of Flannery O'Connor, this list includes her known publications and posthumous collations of her work. Within the entries of the given year, the personal events appear first, followed by publications and awards. Fiction publications are listed first, then essays and book reviews.

1925 Born Mary Flannery O'Connor on March 25th in Savannah, Georgia; only child of Edward Francis O'Connor, and Regina Cline O'Connor.

1930 Appeared in Pathé News Film with pet Bantam chicken that walked forwards and backwards.

1931 Enrolled in parochial school, Savannah.

1938 Moved with family to Milledgeville, Georgia; father ill with disseminated lupus.
Enrolled in Peabody High School, Milledgeville.

1941 Father died of lupus, February 1st.

1942 Graduated from Peabody High School.
Enrolled in Georgia State College for Women, Milledgeville (now known as Georgia College).[1]
Served as editor of the literary quarterly, *The Corinthian*, and art editor of the student newspaper, *The Collonnade*.

1945 Served as feature editor of senior year book.
Graduated from Georgia State College for Women with a B.A. in Social Science.
Dropped "Mary" from name.
Enrolled in Writers' Workshop, State University of Iowa (now the University of Iowa).

1946 Published first short story:

---

[1]By beginning her college education in the summer term and continuing her studies year-round, she was able to obtain her degree in three years.

"The Geranium," *Accent*.[2]
Flannery O'Connor Collection established at Ina Dillard Library, Georgia College.[3]

1947   Began work on her first novel, *Wise Blood*.
       Received Master of Fine Arts degree from the State University of Iowa.

1948   Resided at Yaddo, a writer's colony in Saratoga Springs, New York.
       Engaged Elizabeth McKee as her literary agent.
       Published short stories:
           "The Train," *Sewanee Review*.
           "The Capture," *Mademoiselle* (earlier titled "The Turkey").

1949   Stayed briefly in a New York City apartment house.
       Returned to Milledgeville for an extended visit from March to September.
       Moved to Connecticut farm of Robert and Sally Fitzgerald in September.
       Published short stories:
           "The Heart of the Park," *Partisan Review*.
           "The Woman on the Stairs," *Tomorrow* (later retitled "A Stroke of Good Fortune").
           "The Peeler," *Partisan Review*.

1950   Hospitalized in Atlanta in December with first major attack of lupus.

1951   Moved permanently to Andalusia farm, Milledgeville.

1952   Published first novel:
           Wise Blood.
       Published short story:
           "Enoch and the Gorilla," *New World Writing*.

1953   Published short stories:
           "A Good Man Is Hard to Find," *The Berkeley Book of Modern Writing*.
           "The Life You Save May Be Your Own," *Kenyon Review*.
           "The River," *Sewanee Review*.
           "A Late Encounter with the Enemy," *Harper's Bazaar*.
       Received the *Kenyon Review* Fellowship in Fiction.

---

[2]Full bibliographical information for the published fiction is given in the Bibliography. Publication information for the book reviews is given in Getz, *Flannery O'Connor: Her Life, Library and Book Reviews*, pp. 204-213.

[3]The early collection consisted of fiction pieces from her high school and college days. As her stories appeared in print, copies were added to the collection along with newspaper interviews and articles.

1954 Published short stories:
        "A Circle in the Fire," *Kenyon Review*.
        "A Temple of the Holy Ghost," *Harper's Bazaar*.
        "The Displaced Person," *Sewanee Review*.
      Reappointed Kenyon Fellow.
      Received O. Henry Award, second prize, for "The Life You
        Save May Be Your Own."

1955 Published first collection of short stories:
        A Good Man Is Hard to Find.
      Published short stories:
        "The Artificial Nigger," *Kenyon Review*.
        "Good Country People," *Harper's Bazaar*.
        "You Can't Be Any Poorer Than Dead," *New World Writing*.
      Recieved O. Henry Award, second prize, *The Best American
        Short Stories of 1955*, for "A Circle in the Fire."

1956 Began a series of lecture trips to colleges and universi-
        ties.
      Published short story:
        "Greenleaf," *Kenyon Review*.
      Published first book reviews:
        The Malefactors, by Caroline Gordon.
        The Presence of Grace, by J. F. Powers.
        Two Portraits of St. Thérèse of Lisieux, by Etienne
          Robo.
        Humble Powers, by Paul Horgan.
        Letters from Baron von Hügel to a Niece, by Friedrich
          von Hügel.
        Beyond the Dreams of Avarice, by Russell Kirk.
        The Catholic Companion to the Bible, by Ralph L.
          Woods, ed.
        Meditations Before Mass, by Romano Guardini.
      Received O. Henry Award, *The Best American Short Stories of
        1956*, for "The Artificial Nigger."

1957 Published short story:
        "A View of the Woods," *Partisan Review*.
      Published first essays:
        "The Church and the Fiction Writer," *America*.
        "The Fiction Writer and His Country," *The Living
          Novel*.
      Reviewed:
        The Metamorphic Tradition in Modern Poetry, by Bernet-
          ta Quinn.
        Writings, by Edith Stein.
        Criticism and Censorship, by Walter F. Kerr.
      Received National Institute of Arts and Letters grant.
      Received O. Henry Award, first prize, *The Best American
        Short Stories of 1957*, for "Greenleaf."

1958 Traveled to Lourdes and Rome with mother; audience with
        Pope Pius XII.
      Published short story:
        "The Enduring Chill," *Harper's Bazaar*.
      Reviewed:

      The Transgressor, by Julian Green.
      Patterns in Comparative Religion, by Mircea Eliade.
      American Classics Reconsidered, by Harold C. Gardiner,
         ed.
      Israel and Revelation, by Eric Voeglin.
      Late Dawn, by Elizabeth Vandon.
   Received O. Henry Award, *The Best American Short Stories of
   1958*, for "A View of the Woods."

1959   Published essay:
      "Replies to Two Questions," *Esprit*.
   Reviewed:
      Freud and Religion, by Gregory Zilboorg.
      Temporal and Eternal, by Charles Péguy.
      Harry Vernon at Prep, by Franc Smith.
   Received a grant from the Ford Foundation.

1960   Published second novel:
      The Violent Bear It Away.
   Published short story:
      "The Comforts of Home," *Kenyon Review*.
   Reviewed:
      Jesus Christus: Meditations, by Romano Guardini.
      Mary, Mother of Faith, by Josef Weiger.
      The Pyx, by John Buell.
      Sister Clare, by Loretta Burrough.
      God's Frontier, by J. L. M. Descalzo.
      The Modernity of St. Augustine, by Jean Guitton.
      The Christian Message and Myth, by L. Malavez.
      Christ and Apollo, by William F. Lynch.
      The Son of Man, by François Mauriac.
      Beat on a Damask Drum, by T. K. Martin.
      The Science of the Cross, by Edith Stein.
      Pierre Teilhard de Chardin, by Nicholas Corte.
      Soul and Psyche, by Victor White.
      Christian Initiation, by Louis Bouyer.
      Modern Catholic Thinkers, by A. Robert Caponigri, ed.

1961   Published short stories:
      "Everything That Rises Must Converge," *New World
         Writing*.
      "The Partridge Festival," *Critic*.
   Published essays:
      "Living with a Peacock," *Holiday* (later retitled "The
         King of the Birds").
      "The Novelist and Free Will," *Fresco*.
   Edited:
      Death of a Child (later retitled *Memoir of Mary Ann*).
        Introduction by Flannery O'Connor also published
        separately under the title "The Mystery of Suffer-
        ing."
   Reviewed:
      The Divine Milieu, by Pierre Teilhard de Chardin.
      The Life of St. Catherine of Siena, by Raymond of
        Capua.

The Cardinal Stritch Story, by Marie Cecilia Buehrle.
Leo XIII: A Light from Heaven, by William J. Kiefer.
The Conversion of Augustine, by Romano Guardini.
The Critic (quarterly).
Stop Pushing! by Dan Herr.
Life's Long Journey, by Kenneth Macfarlane Walker.
Selected Letters of Stephen Vincent Benét, by Charles
  Fenton, ed.
The Resurrection, by F. X. Durrwell.
Themes of the Bible, by Jacques Guillet.
The Mediaeval Mystics of England, by Eric Colledge,
  ed.
Freedom, Grace, and Destiny, by Romano Guardini.
The Range of Reason, by Jacques Maritain.
The Bible and the Ancient Near East, by G. E. Wright.
The Old Testament and Modern Study, by H. H. Rowley,
  ed.
The Novelist and the Passion Story, by F. W. Dilli-
  stone.
Teilhard de Chardin, by Oliver A. Rabut.
The Phenomenon of Man, by Pierre Teilhard de Chardin.

1962 Published short story:
        "The Lame Shall Enter First," *Sewanee Review*.
      Reviewed:
        Conversations with Cassandra, by Sister M. Madeleva.
        Christian Faith and Man's Religion, by Marc C. Ebersole.
        Christianity Divided, by Daniel J. Callahan, Heiko A.
          Oberman and Daniel J. O'Hanlon, eds.
        Evidence of Satan in the Modern World, by Léon Christi-
          ani.
        The Georgia Review (quarterly)
        The Conscience of Israel, by Bruce Vawter.
        The Victorian Vision, by Margaret M. Maison.
        Toward the Knowledge of God, by Claude Tresmontant.
        The Cardinal Spellman Story, by Robert I. Gannon.
        The Council, Reform and Reunion, by Hans Küng.
        The Integrating Mind, by William F. Lynch.
        Mystics of Our Times, by Hilda Graef.
        The Catholic in America, by Peter J. Rahill.
      Second printing of *Wise Blood* with "Introduction" by Flan-
        nery O'Connor.
      Received honorary Doctor of Letters, St. Mary's College,
        Notre Dame.

1963 Published short story:
        "Why Do the Heathen Rage?" *Esquire*.
      Published essays:
        "Fiction Is a Subject with a History; It Should Be
          Taught That Way," *The Georgia Bulletin*.
        "The Regional Writer," *Esprit*.
      Reviewed:
        The Bible: Word of God in Words of Men, by Jean Levie.
        Frontiers in American Catholicism, by Walter J. Ong.
        New Men for New Times, by Beatrice Avalos.

> *Seeds of Hope in the Modern World*, by Barry Ulanov.
> *The Wide World, My Parish*, by Yves Congar.
> *Letters from a Traveler*, by Pierre Teilhard de Chardin.
> *The Holiness of Vincent de Paul*, by Jacques Delarue.
> *St. Vincent de Paul*, by Leonard von Matt and Louis
>   Cognet.
> *Saint Vincent de Paul*, by M. V. Woodgate.
> *Faith, Reason and the Gospels*, by John J. Heaney, ed.
> *What is the Bible?* by Henri Daniel-Rops.
> *Image of America*, by Norman Foerster.
> *The Modern God*, by Gustave Weigel.
> *Evangelical Theology*, by Karl Barth.
> *Morte d'Urban*, by J. F. Powers.

Received Honorary Doctor of Letters, Smith College.
Received O. Henry Award, first prize, *Prize Stories of
    1963*, for "Everything That Rises Must Converge."

1964   Underwent abdominal surgery in Spring; lupus reactivated.
       Published short story:
>   "Revelation," *Sewanee Review*.
       Published essay:
>   "The Role of the Catholic Novelist," *Greyfriar*.
       Reviewed:
>   *The Kingdom of God*, by Louis J. Putz, ed.
>   *Prince of Democracy*, by Arline Boucher and John Tehan.
       Printing of *Three by Flannery O'Connor* (contains *Wise Blood,
       A Good Man Is Hard to Find* and *The Violent Bear It
       Away*).
       Died August 3rd at hospital in Milledgeville.

Posthumous Publications,

Collations and Awards

1965   Publication of second collection of short stories:
>   *Everything That Rises Must Converge.*
       Publication of "Parker's Back," *Esquire*.
       Publication of essay:
>   "Some Aspects of the Grotesque in Southern Fiction,"
>   *Cluster Review*.
       O. Henry Award, first prize, *Prize Stories of 1965*, to
       "Revelation."

1966   National Catholic Book Award to *Everything That Rises Must
       Converge*.

1970   Publication of *Mystery and Manners: The Occasional Prose of
           Flannery O'Connor*, by Sally and Robert Fitzgerald, eds.
       Publication of "Wildcat," *North American Review*.
>   "The Barber," *Atlantic*.
       Manuscripts added to the Flannery O'Connor Collection by
       Regina Cline O'Connor.

1971   Publication of *The Complete Stories of Flannery O'Connor*, by
       Robert Giroux, ed.; National Bood Award.

Publication of "The Crop," *Mademoiselle*.

Establishment of the Flannery O'Connor Memorial Room at the Ina Dillard Russell Library, Georgia College.

1974 Substantial portion of personal library holdings given to Georgia College by Regina Cline O'Connor.

1979 Publication of *The Habit of Being: Letters of Flannery O'Connor*, by Sally Fitzgerald, ed.

1980 Publication of previously published but uncollected book reviews in *Flannery O'Connor: Her Life, Library and Book Reviews*, by Lorine M. Getz.

BIBLIOGRAPHY

Adams, Robert Martin. "Fiction Chronicle." *Hudson Review,* 8 (1956), 627-632.

Aherne, C[onsuelo] M[aria]. "Grace, Controversies on." *New Catholic Encyclopedia.* Vol. 6. 1967.

Aristotle. *Poetics.* Trans. Ingram Bywater. New York: Modern Library, 1954.

--------. *The Poetics.* Trans. Preston H. Epps. Chapel Hill: Univ. of North Carolina Press, 1942.

"The Art of the Short Story: Principles and Practice in the United States." In *American Writing Today: Its Independence and Vigor.* Ed. Allen Angoff. New York: New York Univ. Press, 1958, pp. 176-191.

Asals, Frederick. *Flannery O'Connor: The Imagination of Extremity.* Athens: Univ. of Georgia Press, 1982.

--------. "Flannery O'Connor as Novelist: A Defense." *The Flannery O'Connor Bulletin,* 3 (1974), 23-39.

--------. "Flannery O'Connor's 'The Lame Shall Enter First.'" *Mississippi Quarterly,* 23 (1970), 103-120.

--------. "Flannery Row." *Novel,* 4 (1970), 92-96.

--------. "Hawthorne, Mary Ann, and 'The Lame Shall Enter First.'" *The Flannery O'Connor Bulletin,* 2 (1973), 3-18.

--------. "Mythic Dimensions in Flannery O'Connor's 'Greenleaf.'" *Studies in Short Fiction,* 5 (1968), 317-330.

Augustine. *The Confessions.* Trans. Edward B. Pusey. New York: Collier, 1961.

--------. *De nuptiis et concupiscentia (On Marriage and Concupiscence),* in his *Anti-Pelagian Works.* Vol. V of *A Select Library of the Nicene and Post-Nicene Fathers of the Christian Church.* Ed. Philip Schaff. Trans. Peter Holmes et al. Grand Rapids: William B. Eerdmans, 1956, pp. 258-308.

[Baldeschwiler], Sister M. Joselyn. "Thematic Centers in 'The Displaced Person.'" *Studies in Short Fiction,* 1 (1964), 85-92.

Bassan, Maurice. "Flannery O'Connor's Way: Shock, with Moral Intent." *Renascence,* 15 (1963), 195-199, 211.

Baumbach, Jonathan. "The Acid of God's Grace: The Fiction of Flannery O'Connor." *Georgia Review,* 17 (1963), 334-346.

Bercovitch, Sacvan. *The American Puritan Imagination: Essays in Revaluation*. New York: Cambridge Univ. Press, 1974.

Bergup, Berenice. "Themes of Redemptive Grace in the Works of Flannery O'Connor." *The American Benedictine Review*, 21 (1970), 169-191.

Bertrande, Sister. "Four Stories of Flannery O'Connor." *Thought*, 37 (1962), 410-426.

Bliven, Naomi. "Review of *Everything That Rises Must Converge*." *New Yorker*, Sept. 11, 1965, pp. 220-221.

Bornhauser, Fred. "Review of *A Good Man Is Hard to Find* and *The Bride of Innisfallen*." *Shenandoah*, 7, No. 1 (Autumn, 1955), 71-81.

Bowen, Robert O. "Hope vs. Despair in the New Gothic Novel." *Renascence*, 13 (1961), 147-152.

Bradbury, John M. *Renaissance in the South: A Critical History of the Literature, 1920-1960*. Chapel Hill: Univ. of North Carolina Press, 1964.

Brodin, Pierre. *Présences contemporaines: Écrivains Américains d'aujourd'hui*. Paris: Nouvelles Éditions Debresse, 1964, pp. 217-218.

Brown, Peter. *Augustine of Hippo*. London: Faber and Faber, 1967.

Browning, Preston M. *Flannery O'Connor*. Carbondale: Southern Illinois Univ. Press, 1974.

--------. "Flannery O'Connor and the Demonic." *Modern Fiction Studies*, 19 (1973), 29-41.

--------. "Flannery O'Connor and the Grotesque Recovery of the Holy." In *Adversity and Grace: Studies in Recent American Literature*. Ed. Nathan A. Scott. Chicago: Univ. of Chicago Press, 1968, pp. 133-161.

--------. "'Parker's Back': Flannery O'Connor's Iconography of Salvation by Profanity." *Studies in Short Fiction*, 6 (1969), 525-535.

Burke, E[ugene] M. "Grace." *New Catholic Encyclopedia*. Vol. 6. 1967.

Burke, John J. "Convergence of Flannery O'Connor and Chardin." *Renascence*, 19 (1966), 41-47, 52.

Burns, Stuart L. "Flannery O'Connor's *The Violent Bear It Away*: Apotheosis in Failure." *Sewanee Review*, 76 (1968), 319-336.

--------. "Freaks in a Circus Tent: Flannery O'Connor's Christ-Haunted Characters." *The Flannery O'Connor Bulletin*, 1 (1972), 3-23.

Byrd, Turner F. "Ironic Dimension in Flannery O'Connor's 'The Artificial Nigger.'" *Mississippi Quarterly*, 21 (1968), 243-251.

Carlson, Thomas M. "Flannery O'Connor: The Manichaean Dilemma." *Sewanee Review*, 77 (1969), 254-276.

Carter, Thomas H. "Rhetoric and Southern Landscapes." *Accent*, 15 (1955), 293-297.

Charles, Gerda. "Review of *The Violent Bear It Away*." *New Statesman*, 59 (1960), 445-446.

Charles, Norman. "A Lecture." In *The Added Dimension: The Art and Mind of Flannery O'Connor*. Ed. Melvin J. Friedman and Lewis A. Lawson. New York: Fordham Univ. Press, 1966, pp. 269-280.

Cheney, Brainard. "Flannery O'Connor's Campaign for Her Country." *Sewanee Review*, 72 (1964), 555-558.

--------. "Mary Flannery O'Connor." *New Catholic Encyclopedia*. Vol. 10. 1967.

--------. "Miss O'Connor Creates Unusual Humor Out of Ordinary Sin." *Sewanee Review*, 71 (1963), 644-653.

Coffey, Warren. "Flannery O'Connor." *Commentary*, 40, No. 5 (Nov., 1965), 93-99.

Cognet, L[ouis] J[ean]. "Jansenism." *New Catholic Encyclopedia*. Vol. 7. 1967.

Creekmore, Hubert. "A Southern Baptism." *New Leader*, May 30, 1960, pp. 20-21.

Cyvas, Rita. "Redemptive Grace in 'The Comforts of Home.'" Unpublished Manuscript. Cleveland State Univ., 1976.

Daniel, Frank. "A Good Writer Must Set His Book in a Region Which Is Familiar." *Atlanta Journal*, March 28, 1960, p. 27.

Davis, Barnabas. "Flannery O'Connor: Christian Belief in Recent Fiction." *Listening*, 1 (1965), 5-21.

Davis, Joe Lee. "Outraged, or Embarrassed: Review of *Wise Blood* and *The Happy Rural Seat*." *Kenyon Review*, 15 (1953), 320-326.

Degnan, James P. "Review of *Everything That Rises Must Converge*." *The Commonweal*, 82 (1965), 510-511.

Denham, Robert D. "The World of Guilt and Sorrow: Flannery O'Connor's 'Everything That Rises Must Converge.'" *The Flannery O'Connor Bulletin*, 4 (1975), 42-51.

Desmond, John F. "The Lessons of History: Flannery O'Connor's 'Everything That Rises Must Converge.'" *The Flannery O'Connor Bulletin*, 1 (1972), 39-45.

--------. "The Mystery of the Word and the Act: *The Violent Bear It Away*." *The American Benedictine Review*, 24 (1973), 342-347.

Detweiler, Robert. "The Curse of Christ in Flannery O'Connor's Fiction." *Comparative Literature Studies*, 3 (1966), 235-245.

Donner, Robert. "She Writes Powerful Fiction." *Sign*, March, 1961, pp. 46-48.

Dowell, Bob. "The Moment of Grace in the Fiction of Flannery O'Connor." *College English*, 27 (1965), 235-239.

Drake, Robert. "The Bleeding, Stinking, Mad Shadow of Jesus in the Fiction of Flannery O'Connor." *Comparative Literature Studies*, 3 (1966), 183-196.

--------. "Flannery O'Connor and American Literature." *The Flannery O'Connor Bulletin*, 3 (1974), 1-22.

--------. "Hair-Curling Gospel." *The Christian Century*, 82 (1965), 656.

--------. "The Harrowing Evangel of Flannery O'Connor." *The Christian Century*, 81 (1964), 1200-1202.

--------. "Miss O'Connor and the Scandal of Redemption." *Modern Age*, 4 (1960), 428-430.

--------. "The Paradigm of Flannery O'Connor's True Country." *Studies in Short Fiction*, 6 (1969), 433-442.

Driskell, Leon. "'Parker's Back' vs. 'The Partridge Festival': Flannery O'Connor's Critical Choice." *Georgia Review*, 21 (1967), 476-490.

--------, and Joan T. Brittain. *The Eternal Crossroads: The Art of Flannery O'Connor*. Lexington: Univ. of Kentucky Press, 1971.

Driver, Tom F. *Patterns of Grace: Human Experience as Word of God*. San Francisco: Harper and Row, 1977.

Duhamel, P. Albert. "Flannery O'Connor: A Tribute." *Esprit*, 8 (1964), 22-23.

--------. "Flannery O'Connor's Violent View of Reality." *The Catholic World*, 190 (1960), 280-285.

Dunn, Robert J. "The Manuscripts of Flannery O'Connor at Georgia College." *The Flannery O'Connor Bulletin*, 5 (1976), 24-38.

Duprey, Richard A. "Review of *Everything That Rises Must Converge*." *The Catholic World*, 202 (1965), 54.

Eggenschwiler, David. *The Christian Humanism of Flannery O'Connor*. Detroit: Wayne State Univ. Press, 1972.

Elder, Walter. "That Region." *Kenyon Review*, 17 (1955), 661-670.

Engle, Paul. "Insight, Richness, Humor, and Chills." *Chicago Sunday Tribune Magazine of Books*, March 6, 1960, p. 4.

--------, and Martin Hansford, eds. "Introduction." *Prize Stories 1955: The O. Henry Awards*. Garden City, N.Y.: Doubleday, 1955, pp. 9-12.

Esty, William. "In America, Intellectual Bomb Shelters." *The Commonweal*, 68 (1958), 586-588.

Fahey, William A. "Flannery O'Connor's 'Parker's Back.'" *Renascence*, 20 (1968), 162-164, 166.

Farnham, James F. "The Essential Flannery O'Connor." *Cross Currents*, 15 (1965), 376-378.

--------. "Flannery O'Connor and the Incarnation of Mystery." *Cross Currents*, 20 (1970), 252-256.

--------. "The Grotesque in Flannery O'Connor." *America*, 105 (1961), 277, 280-281.

Feeley, Kathleen. *Flannery O'Connor: Voice of the Peacock*. New Brunswick, N.J.: Rutgers Univ. Press, 1972.

--------. Unpublished lecture. Georgia College, Milledgeville, Georgia. July 12, 1975.

Ferris, Sumner J. "The Outside and the Inside: Flannery O'Connor's *The Violent Bear It Away*." *Critique: Studies in Modern Fiction*, 3, No. 2 (1960), 11-19.

Fiedler, Leslie A. *Love and Death in the American Novel*. New York: Criterion Books, 1960.

Fitzgerald, Robert S. "The Countryside and the True Country." *Sewanee Review*, 70 (1962), 380-394.

--------. "Introduction," In Flannery O'Connor, *Everything That Rises Must Converge*. New York: Noonday Press [1965].

--------, and Sally Fitzgerald, eds. *Mystery and Manners: The Occasional Prose of Flannery O'Connor*. New York: Farrar, Straus and Giroux, 1970.

Fitzgerald, Sally. "Assumption and Experience: Flannery O'Connor's 'A Temple of the Holy Ghost.'" *Cross Currents*, 31 (Winter, 1981-82), 423-432.

--------. "The Habit of Being." *The Flannery O'Connor Bulletin*, 6 (1977), 5-16.

--------. Unpublished lecture, Flannery O'Connor Symposium, Georgia College, Milledgeville, Georgia. April 3, 1977.

--------, ed. *The Habit of Being: Letters of Flannery O'Connor*.
    New York: Farrar, Straus and Giroux, 1979.

Flores-Del Prado, Wilma. "Flannery O'Connor's Gallery of Freaks."
    Saint Louis Univ. Research Journal, 2 (1971), 463-514.

Fowler, Doreen Ferlaino. "Mrs. Chestny's Saving Graces." *The
    Flannery O'Connor Bulletin*, 6 (1977), 99-106.

Friedman, Melvin J., and Lewis A. Lawson, eds. *The Added Dimen-
    sion: The Art and Mind of Flannery O'Connor*. New York:
    Fordham Univ. Press, 1966.

"Frustrated Preacher: Review of *Wise Blood*." *Newsweek*, May 19,
    1952, pp. 114-115.

Frye, Northrop. *Anatomy of Criticism: Four Essays*. Princeton,
    N.J.: Princeton Univ. Press, 1957; rpt. Princeton Paperback,
    1971.

--------. *The Secular Scripture: A Study of the Structure of Ro-
    mance*. Cambridge: Harvard Univ. Press, 1976.

Gable, Mariella. "But First It Must Rise." *The Critic*, 23,
    No. 6 (June-July, 1965), 58-60.

--------. "Ecumenic Core in Flannery O'Connor's Fiction." *The
    American Benedictine Review*, 15 (1964), 127-143.

Gardiner, Harold C. "Flannery O'Connor's Clarity of Vision." In
    The Added Dimension: The Art and Mind of Flannery O'Connor.
    Ed. Melvin J. Friedman and Lewis A. Lawson. New York: Ford-
    ham Univ. Press, 1966, pp. 184-195.

--------. "A Tragic New Image of Man." *America*, 102 (1960), 682-
    683.

Geher, Istvan. "Flannery O'Connor," in Flannery O'Connor, *Mind-
    en Összefut*. Ed. and trans. Istvan Geher. Budapest: Európa
    Könyvkiadó, 1968, pp. 255-267.

Getz, Lorine M. *Flannery O'Connor: Her Life, Library and Book
    Reviews*. New York and Toronto: Edwin Mellen, 1980.

Giroux, Robert. "Introduction," in Flannery O'Connor, *The Com-
    plete Stories*. New York: Farrar, Straus and Giroux, 1971.

"God Breaks Through: Review of *Everything That Rises Must Con-
    verge* and *A Pile of Stones*." *America*, 112 (1965), 821-822.

Golden, Robert E., and Mary C. Sullivan. *Flannery O'Connor and
    Caroline Gordon: A Reference Guide*. Boston: G. K. Hall,
    1977.

Gordon, Caroline. "Flannery O'Connor's *Wise Blood*." *Critique: Studies in Modern Fiction*, 2, No. 2 (Fall, 1958), 3-10.

--------. "Heresy in Dixie." *Sewanee Review*, 76 (1968), 263-297.

--------. "With a Glitter of Evil." *New York Times Book Review*, June 12, 1955, p. 5.

--------, and Allen Tate, eds. *The House of Fiction: An Anthology of the Short Story with Commentary*. 2nd ed. New York: Scribners, 1960.

Gossett, Louise Y. "The Test by Fire: Flannery O'Connor," in her *Violence in Recent Southern Fiction*. Durham, N.C.: Duke Univ. Press, 1965, pp. 75-97.

--------. *Violence in Recent Southern Fiction*. Durham, N.C.: Duke Univ. Press, 1965.

Goyen, William. "Unending Vengeance." *New York Times Book Review*, May 18, 1952, p. 4.

"Grace Through Nature: Review of *Everything That Rises Must Converge*." *Newsweek*, May 31, 1965, p. 85.

"Grave and Gay." *Times Literary Supplement*, Sept. 2, 1955, p. 505.

Guardini, Romano. *The Conversion of Augustine*. Trans. Elinor C. Briefs. Westminster, Md.: Newman, 1960.

--------. *The Faith and Modern Man*. Trans. Charlotte E. Forsyth. Chicago: Henry Regnery, 1952; rpt. 1965.

--------. *Freedom, Grace, and Destiny: Three Chapters in the Interpretation of Existence*. Trans. John Murray. New York: Pantheon, 1961.

Gunn, Giles B., ed. *Literature and Religion*. London: SCM Press, 1971.

Hardwick, Elizabeth. "Flannery O'Connor, 1925-1964." *New York Review of Books*, Oct. 8, 1964, pp. 21, 23.

Hart, Jane. "Strange Earth, the Stories of Flannery O'Connor." *Georgia Review*, 12 (1958), 215-222.

Hassan, Ihab. *Radical Innocence: Studies in the Contempory Novel*. New York: Harper and Row, 1961.

Hawkes, John. "Flannery O'Connor: A Tribute." *Esprit*, 8 (1964), 30.

--------. "Flannery O'Connor's Devil." *Sewanee Review*, 70 (1962), 395-407.

--------. "John Hawkes. An Interview." *Wisconsin Studies in Contemporary Literature*, 6 (1965), 141-155.

Hays, Peter L. "Dante, Tobit, and 'The Artificial Nigger.'" *Studies in Short Fiction*, 5 (1968), 263-268.

Hegarty, Charles M. "God in Flannery O'Connor's Fiction." Unpublished lecture, Modern Language Association, Chicago. Dec. 29, 1973.

--------. "A Man Though Not Yet a Whole One: Mr. Shiftlet's Genesis." *The Flannery O'Connor Bulletin*, 1 (1972), 66-71.

Hendin, Josephine. *The World of Flannery O'Connor*. Bloomington: Indiana Univ. Press, 1970.

Hicks, Granville. "A Cold, Hard Look at Humankind." *Saturday Review*, May 29, 1965, pp. 23-24.

--------. "Flannery O'Connor: A Tribute." *Esprit*, 8 (1964), 30.

--------. "Holy Kind of Horror." *Saturday Review*, July 2, 1966, pp. 21-22.

--------. "Living with Books." *New Leader*, August 15, 1955, p. 17.

--------. "Southern Gothic with a Vengeance." *Saturday Review*, Feb. 27, 1960, p. 18.

Hines, Melissa. "Grotesque Conversions and Critical Piety." *The Flannery O'Connor Bulletin*, 6 (1977), 17-35.

Hirsch, E. D., Jr. *The Aims of Interpretation*. Chicago: Univ. of Chicago Press, 1976.

Hoffman, Frederick J. *The Imagination's New Beginning: Theology and Modern Literature*. Notre Dame, Ind.: Univ. of Notre Dame Press, 1967.

--------. "James Agee and Flannery O'Connor: The Religious Consciousness," in his *The Art of Southern Fiction*. Carbondale: Southern Illinois Univ. Press, 1967, pp. 74-95.

--------. "The Search for Redemption: Flannery O'Connor's Fiction." In *The Added Dimension: The Art and Mind of Flannery O'Connor*. Ed. Melvin J. Friedman and Lewis A. Lawson. New York: Fordham Univ. Press, 1966, pp. 32-48.

Holman, C. Hugh. "Her Rue with a Difference: Flannery O'Connor and the Southern Literary Tradition." In *The Added Dimension: The Art and Mind of Flannery O'Connor*. Ed. Melvin J. Friedman and Lewis A. Lawson. New York: Fordham Univ. Press, 1966, pp. 73-87.

Hoobler, Thomas. "Review of *Everything That Rises Must Converge.*" *Ave Maria*, 102 (1965), 376-378.

Hopkins, Mary Frances. "Julian's Mother." *The Flannery O'Connor Bulletin*, 7 (1978), 114-115.

Hopper, Stanley Romaine, ed. *Spiritual Problems in Contemporary Literature*. New York: Harper and Brothers, 1952.

Howe, Irving. "Flannery O'Connor's Stories." *New York Review of Books*, Sept. 30, 1965, pp. 16-17.

Hughes, Riley. "Review of *A Good Man Is Hard to Find.*" *The Catholic World*, 181 (1955), 66-67.

Hugo, John J. *St. Augustine on Nature, Sex, and Marriage*. Chicago: Scepter, 1969.

Hunter, Anna C. "Review of *The Violent Bear It Away.*" *Savannah Morning News Magazine*, Feb. 21, 1960, p. 13.

Hyman, Stanley Edgar. *Flannery O'Connor*. Minneapolis: Univ. of Minnesota Press, 1966; rpt. in Leonard Unger, ed., *American Writers: A Collection of Literary Biographies*. New York: Charles Scribner's Sons, 1974, III, 337-360.

--------. "Flannery O'Connor's Tattooed Christ." *New Leader*, May 10, 1965, pp. 9-10.

Ingram, Forrest L. "O'Connor's Seven-Story Cycle." *The Flannery O'Connor Bulletin*, 2 (1973), 19-28.

Jacobsen, Josephine. "A Catholic Quartet." *The Christian Scholar*, 47 (1964), 139-154.

Jeremy, Sister. "*The Violent Bear It Away*: A Linguistic Education." *Renascence*, 17 (1964), 11-16.

Joselyn, Sister M. See Baldeschwiler, Sister M. Joselyn.

Judge, John F. "The Man Under the Microscope: A Look at 'The Displaced Person.'" *Esprit*, 8 (1964), 65.

Kann, Jean Marie. "Everything That Rises Must Converge." *The Catholic World*, 204 (1966), 154-159.

Kazin, Alfred. *Bright Book of Life: American Novelists and Storytellers form Hemingway to Mailer*. Boston: Little, Brown, 1973.

Kellogg, Gene. "The Catholic Novel in Convergence." *Thought*, 45 (1970), 265-296.

--------. *The Vital Tradition: The Catholic Novel in a Period of Convergence*. Chicago: Loyola Univ. Press, 1970.

Kirkland, William. "Flannery O'Connor, the Person and the Writer." *East-West Review*, 3 (1967), 159-163.

Kropf, C. R. "Theme and Setting in 'A Good Man Is Hard to Find.'" *Renascence*, 24 (1972), 177-180, 206.

LaFarge, Oliver. "Manic Gloom." *Saturday Review*, May 24, 1952, p. 22.

Lawson, Lewis A. "Flannery O'Connor and the Grotesque: *Wise Blood*." *Renascence*, 17 (1965), 137-147, 156.

--------. "The Grotesque in Recent Southern Fiction." In *Patterns of Commitment in American Literature*. Ed. Marston LaFrance. Toronto: Univ. of Toronto Press, 1967, pp. 165-179.

LeClezio, J. M. G. "L'Univers de Flannery O'Connor." *Nouvelle Revue Française*, 13 (1965), 488-493.

Lensing, George. "De Chardin's Ideas in Flannery O'Connor." *Renascence*, 18 (1966), 171-175.

Lewis, R. W. B. "Eccentrics' Pilgrimage." *Hudson Review*, 6 (1953), 144-150.

Lotz, J[ohannes] B. "Nihilismus." *Lexikon für Theologie und Kirche*. Vol. 7. 1962.

Lynch, William F. *Christ and Apollo: The Dimensions of the Literary Imagination*. New York: Sheed and Ward, 1960.

McCarthy, John F. "Human Intelligence Versus Divine Truth: The Intellectual in Flannery O'Connor's Works." *English Journal*, 55 (1966), 1143-1148.

McCown, Robert. "Flannery O'Connor and the Reality of Sin." *The Catholic World*, 188 (1959), 285-291.

McCullagh, James C. "Aspects of Jansenism in Flannery O'Connor's *Wise Blood*." *Studies in the Humanities*, 3, No. 1 (Oct., 1972), 12-16.

--------. "Symbolism and the Religious Aesthetic: Flannery O'Connor's *Wise Blood*." *The Flannery O'Connor Bulletin*, 2 (1973), 43-58.

McFague, Sallie. See TeSelle, Sallie McFague.

McFarland, Dorothy Tuck. *Flannery O'Connor*. New York: Frederick Ungar, 1976.

McKenna, S[tephen] J[oseph]. "Pelagius and Pelagianism." *New Catholic Encyclopedia*. Vol. 11. 1967.

--------. "Semi-Pelagianism." *New Catholic Encyclopedia*. Vol. 13. 1967.

Mackey, James P. *The Grace of God, the Response of Man: A Study in Basic Theology*. Albany, N.Y.: Magi Books, 1966.

McKulik, Ben. "Flannery O'Connor as a Reader of Her Own Fiction: The Medieval Consciousness in the Modern World." Unpublished lecture, Modern Language Association, Chicago. Dec. 29, 1973.

Macquarrie, John. *Principles of Christian Theology*. 2nd ed. New York: Charles Scribner's Sons, 1977.

Maida, Patricia Dinneen. "'Convergence' in Flannery O'Connor's 'Everything That Rises Must Converge.'" *Studies in Short Fiction*, 7 (1970), 549-555.

Male, Roy R. "The Two Versions of 'The Displaced Person.'" *Studies in Short Fiction*, 7 (1970), 450-457.

Malin, Irving. "Flannery O'Connor and the Grotesque." In *The Added Dimension: The Art and Mind of Flannery O'Connor*. Ed. Melvin J. Friedman and Lewis A. Lawson. New York: Fordham Univ. Press, 1966, pp. 108-122.

--------. *New American Gothic*. Carbondale: Southern Illinois Univ. Press, 1962.

Maritain, Jacques. *Art and Scholasticism, and The Frontiers of Poetry*. Trans. Joseph W. Evans. New York: Charles Scribner's Sons, 1962.

--------. *The Range of Reason*. New York: Charles Scribner's Sons, 1942; rpt. 1952.

--------. *The Responsibility of the Artist*. New York: Charles Scribner's Sons, 1960.

Marks, W. S. "Advertisements for Grace: Flannery O'Connor's 'A Good Man Is Hard to Find.'" *Studies in Short Fiction*, 4 (1966), 19-27.

Martin, Carter. "Comedy and Humor in Flannery O'Connor's Fiction." *The Flannery O'Connor Bulletin*, 4 (1975), 1-12.

--------. *The True Country: Themes in the Fiction of Flannery O'Connor*. Nashville: Vanderbilt Univ. Press, 1969.

Matteucci, B[envenuto]. "Jansenistic Piety." *New Catholic Ency-
     clopedia.* Vol. 7. 1967.

May, John R. "Flannery O'Connor and the New Hermeneutic." *The
     Flannery O'Connor Bulletin,* 2 (1973), 29-43.

--------. *The Pruning Word: The Parables of Flannery O'Connor.*
     Notre Dame, Ind.: Univ. of Notre Dame Press, 1976.

--------. "*The Violent Bear It Away*: The Meaning of the Title."
     The Flannery O'Connor Bulletin, 2 (1973), 83-86.

Mayer, David R. "Apologia for the Imagination: Flannery O'Con-
     nor's 'A Temple of the Holy Ghost.'" *Studies in Short Fic-
     tion,* 11 (1974), 147-152.

--------. "*The Violent Bear It Away*: Flannery O'Connor's Sha-
     man." *The Southern Literary Journal,* 4, No. 2 (Spring,
     1972), 41-54.

Mayhew, Leonard F. X. "Flannery O'Connor's People: Authentic and
     Universal." *The Georgia Bulletin,* Aug. 6, 1964, p. 7.

Mellard, James M. "Violence and Belief in Mauriac and O'Connor."
     Renascence, 26 (1974), 158-168.

Mercier, Vivien. "Sex, Success and Salvation." *Hudson Review,*
     13 (1960), 449-456.

Merton, Thomas. "Flannery O'Connor: A Prose Elegy," in his *Raids
     on the Unspeakable.* New York: New Directions, 1966, pp. 41-
     42.

--------. "Flannery O'Connor: A Tribute." *Esprit,* 8 (1964), 36.

--------. "The Other Side of Despair: Notes on Christian Existen-
     tialism." *The Critic,* 24, No. 2 (Oct.-Nov., 1965), 12-23.

Miller, James E. *Quests Surd and Absurd: Essays in American Lit-
     erature.* Chicago: Univ. of Chicago Press, 1967.

Millichap, Joseph R. "The Pauline 'Old Man' in Flannery O'Con-
     nor's 'The Comforts of Home.'" *Studies in Short Fiction,* 11
     (1974), 96-99.

Mizener, Arthur. "Some Kinds of Modern Novel." *Sewanee Review,*
     69 (1961), 154-164.

Montgomery, Marion. "Flannery O'Connor and the Natural Man."
     Mississippi Quarterly, 21 (1968), 235-242.

--------. "O'Connor and Teilhard de Chardin: The Problem of
     Evil." *Renascence,* 22 (1969), 34-42.

--------. "The Sense of Violation: Notes Toward a Definition of 'Southern' Fiction." *Georgia Review*, 19 (1965), 278-287.

--------. "Vision and the Eye for Detail in Poe and O'Connor." *The Flannery O'Connor Bulletin*, 6 (1977), 36-46.

Muller, Gilbert H. "The City of Woe: Flannery O'Connor's 'The Artificial Nigger.'" *Georgia Review*, 23 (1969), 206-213.

--------. *Nightmares and Visions: Flannery O'Connor and the Catholic Grotesque*. Athens: Univ. of Georgia Press, 1972.

--------. "*The Violent Bear It Away*: Moral and Dramatic Sense." *Renascence*, 22 (1969), 17-25.

"Nihilism." *Encyclopedia Britannica: Micropaedia*. Vol. 7. 1964.

Nyren, Dorothy. "Review of *The Violent Bear It Away*." *Library Journal*, 85 (1960), 146.

Oates (Smith), Joyce Carol. "Ritual and Violence in Flannery O'Connor." *Thought*, 41 (1966), 545-560.

--------. "The Visionary Art of Flannery O'Connor," in her *New Heaven, New Earth: The Visionary Experience in Literature*. New York: Vanguard Press, 1974, pp. 141-176.

O'Brien, John T. "The Un-Christianity of Flannery O'Connor." *Listening*, 6 (1971), 71-82.

O'Connor, Flannery. *The Complete Stories*. Ed. Robert Giroux. New York: Farrar, Straus and Giroux, 1971.
    Includes:
    "The Geranium," pp. 3-14.
    "The Barber," pp. 15-25.
    "Wildcat," pp. 26-32.
    "The Crop," pp. 33-41.
    "The Turkey," pp. 42-53.
    "The Train," pp. 54-62.
    "The Peeler," pp. 63-80.
    "The Heart of the Park," pp. 81-94.
    "A Stroke of Good Fortune," pp. 95-107.
    "Enoch and the Gorilla," pp. 108-116.
    "A Good Man Is Hard to Find," pp. 117-133.
    "A Late Encounter with the Enemy," pp. 134-144.
    "The Life You Save May Be Your Own," pp. 145-156.
    "The River," pp. 157-174.
    "A Circle in the Fire." pp. 175-193.
    "The Displaced Person," pp. 194-235.
    "A Temple of the Holy Ghost," pp. 236-248.
    "The Artificial Nigger," pp. 249-270.
    "Good Country People," pp. 271-291.
    "You Can't Be Any Poorer Than Dead," pp. 292-310.
    "Greenleaf," pp. 311-334.

"A View of the Woods," pp. 335-356.
"The Enduring Chill," pp. 357-382.
"The Comforts of Home," pp. 383-404.
"Everything That Rises Must Converge," pp. 405-420.
"The Partridge Festival," pp. 421-444.
"The Lame Shall Enter First," pp. 445-482.
"Why Do the Heathen Rage?" pp. 483-487.
"Revelation," pp. 488-509.
"Parker's Back," pp. 510-530.
"Judgement Day," pp. 531-550.

————————. *The Habit of Being: Letters of Flannery O'Connor*. Ed.
     Sally Fitzgerald. New York: Farrar, Straus and Giroux, 1979.

————————. *Mystery and Manners: Occasional Prose*. Ed. Sally and
     Robert Fitzgerald. New York: Farrar, Straus and Cudahy,
     1961; rpt. New York: Noonday Press, 1970.

————————. *Three by Flannery O'Connor*. New York: New American
     Library [c. 1963].
     Includes:
     Wise Blood, pp. 7-126.
     A Good Man Is Hard to Find, pp. 127-299.
     The Violent Bear It Away, pp. 301-447.

O'Connor, William Van. "Flannery O'Connor: A Tribute." *Esprit*,
     8 (1964), 37-39.

————————. "The Grotesque: An American Genre," in his *The Gro-
     tesque: An American Genre, and Other Essays*. Carbondale:
     Southern Illinois Univ. Press, 1962, pp. 3-19.

"Of Ultimate Things: Review of *Everything That Rises Must Con-
     verge*." *Time*, June 4, 1965, p. 92.

O'Grady, John F. *Christian Anthropology: A Meaning for Human
     Life*. New York: Paulist Press, 1976.

Orvell, Miles. *Invisible Parade: The Fiction of Flannery O'Con-
     nor*. Philadelphia: Temple Univ. Press, 1972.

Otto, Rudolf. *The Idea of the Holy: An Inquiry into the Non-
     Rational Factor in the Idea of the Divine and Its Relation
     to the Rational* (1923). Trans. John W. Harvey. New York:
     Oxford Univ. Press, 1973.

Owsley, Frank Lawrence. "The Irrepressible Conflict." In *I'll
     Take My Stand: The South and the Agrarian Tradition* (1930),
     by Twelve Southerners. New York: Harper and Brothers, 1962,
     pp. 61-91.

Peden, William. *The American Short Story: Front Line in the Na-
     tional Defense of Literature*. Boston: Houghton-Mifflin,
     1964.

Phillips, Robert. "The Descent of the Dove: Review of *Everything That Rises Must Converge*." *The North American Review*, 250, No. 2 (May, 1965), 53-54.

Pierce, Constance. "The Mechanical World of 'Good Country People.'" *The Flannery O'Connor Bulletin*, 5 (1976), 30-38.

Praz, Mario. "Racconti del Sud." *Studi Americani*, 2 (1956), 207-218.

Prescott, Orville. "Review of *A Good Man Is Hard to Find*." *New York Times*, June 10, 1955, p. 23.

--------. "Review of *The Violent Bear It Away*." *New York Times*, Feb. 24, 1960, p. 35.

Pryce-Jones, Alan. "A Poignant Knowledge of the Dark." *New York Herald Tribune*, May 25, 1965, p. 23.

Quinn, Bernetta. "Flannery O'Connor, A Realist of Distances." In *The Added Dimension: The Art and Mind of Flannery O'Connor*. Ed. Melvin J. Friedman and Lewis A. Lawson. New York: Fordham Univ. Press, 1966, pp. 157-183.

--------. "View from a Rock: The Fiction of Flannery O'Connor and J. F. Powers." *Critique: Studies in Modern Fiction*, 2, No. 2 (Fall, 1958), 19-27.

Quinn, Thomas. "Lewis and O'Connor: Prophets of the Added Dimension." *Report*, Jan., 1967, pp. 32-33.

Rahner, Karl. "Concerning the Relationship of Nature and Grace," in his *Theological Investigations*. Vol. 1. Trans. Cornelius Ernst. Baltimore: Helicon, 1961, pp. 297-317.

--------. "Nature and Grace," in his *Theological Investigations*. Vol. 4. Trans. Kevin Smyth. London: Darton, Longman and Todd, 1966, pp. 165-188.

--------. "Reflections on the Experience of Grace," in his *Theological Investigations*. Vol. 3. Trans. Karl-H. and Boniface Kruger. London: Darton, Longman and Todd, 1967, pp. 86-90.

--------. "The Theology of the Symbol," in his *Theological Investigations*. Vol. 4. Trans. Kevin Smyth. London: Darton, Longman and Todd, 1966, pp. 221-252.

--------, ed. *Encyclopedia of Theology: The Concise Sacramentum Mundi*. New York: Seabury, 1975.

Reed, John Shelton. *The Enduring South: Subcultural Persistence in Mass Society*. Chapel Hill: Univ. of North Carolina Press, 1974.

Regan, C[ronin]. "Grace and Nature." *New Catholic Encyclopedia*. Vol. 6. 1967.

Reichert, John. *Making Sense of Literature*. Chicago: Univ. of Chicago Press, 1977.

Reiter, Robert E., ed. *Flannery O'Connor*. St. Louis: B. Herder, 1968.

"Review of *A Good Man Is Hard to Find*." *Bookmark*, 14 (1955), 216.

"Review of *A Good Man Is Hard to Find*." *New Yorker*, June 18, 1955, p. 93.

"Review of *A Good Man Is Hard to Find*." *Time*, June 6, 1955, p. 114.

"Review of *The Violent Bear It Away*." *Booklist*, 56 (1960), 478.

"Review of *The Violent Bear It Away*." *New Yorker*, March 19, 1960, p. 179.

"Review of *Wise Blood*." *Kirkus*, 19 (1952), 252.

"Review of *Wise Blood*." *United States Quarterly Book Review*, 8 (1952), 256.

Ries, J[ulien Camille]. "Manichaeism." *New Catholic Encyclopedia*. Vol. 9. 1967.

Rondet, Henri. *The Grace of Christ* (1948). Trans. and ed. Tad W. Guzie. New York: Newman, 1966.

Rosenberger, Coleman. "In a Bizarre Backcountry." *New York Herald Tribune Book Review*, Feb. 28, 1960, p. 13.

Rosenfield, Claire. "The Shadow Within: The Conscious and Unconscious Use of the Double." *Daedalus*, 92 (1963), 326-344.

Ross-Bryant, Lynn. *Imagination and the Life of the Spirit*. Chico, Calif.: Scholars Press, 1981.

Rubin, Louis D. *The Curious Death of the Novel: Essays in American Literature*. Baton Rouge: Louisiana State Univ. Press, 1967.

--------. "Flannery O'Connor and the Bible Belt." In *The Added Dimension: The Art and Mind of Flannery O'Connor*. Ed. Melvin J. Friedman and Lewis A. Lawson. New York: Fordham Univ. Press, 1966, pp. 49-72.

--------. "Flannery O'Connor (1925-1964)," in his *A Bibliographical Guide to the Study of Southern Literature*. Baton

Rouge: Louisiana State Univ. Press, 1969, pp. 250-253.

--------. "Flannery O'Connor's Company of Southerners: Or 'The Artificial Nigger' Read as Fiction Rather Than Theology." *The Flannery O'Connor Bulletin*, 6 (1977), 47-71.

--------. "Southerners and Jews." *Southern Review*, 2 (1966), 697-713.

--------. "Two Ladies of the South." *Sewannee Review*, 63 (1955), 671-681.

--------, et al. "Recent Southern Fiction: A Panel Discussion with Katherine Anne Porter, Flannery O'Connor, Caroline Gordon, Madison Jones, and Louis D. Rubin, Moderator." *Bulletin of Wesleyan College*, 41 (1961), 2-16.

--------, and Robert D. Jacobs, eds. *South: Modern Southern Literature in Its Cultural Setting.* Garden City, N.Y.: Doubleday, 1961; rpt. 1974.

Ruland, Vernon. *Horizons of Criticism: An Assessment of Religious-Literary Options.* Chicago: American Library, 1975.

Russel, R[obert] P[hilip]. "Augustinianism." *New Catholic Encyclopedia.* Vol. 1. 1967.

--------. "Augustinianism, Theological School of." *New Catholic Encyclopedia.* Vol. 1. 1967.

Rutherford, Marjory. "Georgia Author Scores Again: Review of *The Violent Bear It Away.*" *Atlanta Journal and Constitution*, Feb. 28, 1960, p. 2-e.

Schott, Webster. "Flannery O'Connor, Faith's Stepchild." *Nation*, Sept. 13, 1965, pp. 142-144.

--------. "The Struggle of Ideals Is Reality." *Kansas City Star*, March 5, 1960, p.7.

Scott, Nathan A. *The Broken Center: Studies in the Theological Horizon of Modern Literature.* New Haven: Yale Univ. Press, 1966.

--------. "Flannery O'Connor's Testimony: The Pressure of Glory." In *The Added Dimension: The Art and Mind of Flannery O'Connor.* Ed. Melvin J. Friedman and Lewis A. Lawson. New York: Fordham Univ. Press, 1966, pp. 138-156.

--------. *Modern Literature and the Religious Frontier.* New York: Harper and Brothers, 1958.

--------. *Negative Capability: Studies in the New Literature and the Religious Situation.* New Haven: Yale Univ. Press,

1969.

Scott, Wilbur S. *Five Approaches of Literary Criticism*. New
    York: Macmillan, 1962.

Scouten, Kenneth. "The Mythological Dimensions of Five of Flan-
    nery O'Connor's Works." *The Flannery O'Connor Bulletin*, 2
    (1973), 59-72.

Sessions, William. "Flannery O'Connor: A Memoir." *The National
    Catholic Reporter*, Oct. 28, 1964, p. 9.

Shear, Walter. "Flannery O'Connor . . . Character and Character-
    ization." *Renascence*, 20 (1968), 140-146.

Shinn, Thelma J. "Flannery O'Connor and the Violence of Grace."
    Contemporary Literature, 9 (1968), 58-73.

Shloss, Carol. *Flannery O'Connor's Dark Comedies: The Limits of
    Inference*. Baton Rouge and London: Louisiana State Univ.
    Press, 1980.

Smith, J. Oates. See Oates (Smith), Joyce Carol.

Snow, Ollye Tine. "The Functional Gothic of Flannery O'Connor."
    Southwest Review, 50 (1965), 286-299.

Solmsen, Friedrich. "Introduction," in Aristotle, *Rhetoric and
    Poetics*. New York: Modern Library, 1954.

Spiller, Robert, ed. "Flannery O'Connor," in his *Literary His-
    tory of the United States*. 4th ed. New York: Macmillan,
    1974, pp. 1363-1364.

Spivey, Ted R. "Flannery O'Connor: A Tribute." *Esprit*, 8
    (1964), 46, 48.

--------. "Flannery O'Connor: Georgia's Theological Storyteller."
    In *The Humanities in the Contemporary South*. School of Arts
    and Sciences Research Paper No. 17. Atlanta: Georgia State
    College, 1968, pp. 19-28.

--------. "Flannery O'Connor's View of God and Man." *Studies
    in Short Fiction*, 1 (1964), 200-206.

--------. "Flannery O'Connor's South: Don Quixote Rides Again."
    The Flannery O'Connor Bulletin, 1 (1972), 46-53.

Stallings, Sylvia. "Flannery O'Connor: A New Shining Talent
    Among Our Storytellers." *New York Herald Tribune Book
    Review*, June 5, 1955, p. 1.

--------. "Young Writer with a Bizarre Tale to Tell." *New York
    Herald Tribune Book Review*, May 18, 1952, p. 3.

Steggert, Frank X. "Review of *A Good Man Is Hard to Find*." *Books on Trial*, 14 (1955), 187.

Stelzmann, Rainulf. "Shock and Orthodoxy: An Interpretation of Flannery O'Connor's Novels and Stories." *Xavier Univ. Studies*, 2 (1963), 4-21.

Stephens, Martha. *The Question of Flannery O'Connor*. Baton Rouge: Louisiana State Univ. Press, 1973.

Stevens, Clifford. "The Christianity of Flannery O'Connor." *Our Sunday Visitor*, Nov. 7, 1971, pp. 1, 4.

Stewart, Randall. *American Literature and Christian Doctrine*. Baton Rouge: Louisiana State Univ. Press, 1958.

Stone, Edward. *Voices of Despair: Four Motifs in American Literature*. Athens: Ohio Univ. Press, 1966.

Sullivan, Bede. "Flannery O'Connor and the Dialogue Decade." *Catholic Library World*, 31 (1960), 518, 521.

--------. "Prophet in the Wilderness." *Today*, March, 1960, pp. 36-37.

Sullivan, Kathleen. "Review of *The Violent Bear It Away*." *Fonthill Dial*, 37 (1960), 38.

Sullivan, Walter. "The Achievement of Flannery O'Connor." *Southern Humanities Review*, 2 (1968), 303-309.

--------. "Flannery O'Connor, Sin and Grace: *Everything That Rises Must Converge*." *The Hollins Critic*, 2 (1965), 1-8, 10.

Taillefer, Anne. "A Memoir of Flannery O'Connor." *Catholic Worker*, Dec., 1964, pp. 2, 7.

Tate, Allen. "Flannery O'Connor: A Tribute." *Esprit*, 8 (1964), 48-49.

--------. "Remarks on the Southern Religion." In *I'll Take My Stand: The South and the Agrarian Tradition* (1930), by Twelve Southerners. New York: Harper and Brothers, 1962, pp. 155-175.

Tate, James O. "The Uses of Banality." *The Flannery O'Connor Bulletin*, 4 (1975), 13-24.

TeSelle, Sallie McFague. *Speaking in Parables: A Study in Metaphor and Theology*. Philadelphia: Fortress, 1975.

Thomas Aquinas. *On the Truth of The Catholic Church: Summa Contra Gentiles*. 5 vols. Trans. Anton C. Pegis et al. Garden

City, N.Y.: Doubleday Image, 1955-1957.

--------. *Summa Theologiae*. [Trans. Dominican Friars.] 60
vols. New York: McGraw-Hill, 1963.

Thomson, Philip. *The Grotesque*. London: Methuen, 1972.

Townend, Joseph C. "The Inner Country: Design in 'The Lame Shall
Enter First.'" *Esprit*, 8 (1964), 70.

Trowbridge, Clinton W. "The Symbolic Vision of Flannery O'Connor: Patterns of Imagery in *The Violent Bear It Away*." *Sewanee Review*, 76 (1968), 298-318.

Turnell, Martin. *Modern Literature and Christian Faith*. Westminster, Md.: Newman, 1961.

Twelve Southerners. "Introduction: A Statement of Principles,"
in their *I'll Take My Stand: The South and the Agrarian Tradition* (1930). New York: Harper and Brothers, 1962.

Vande Kieft, Ruth M. "Judgment in the Fiction of Flannery O'Connor." *Sewanee Review*, 76 (1968), 337-356.

Voss, Victor. "A Study in Sin." *Esprit*, 8 (1964), 60-62.

Wakeman, John, ed. "Flannery O'Connor," in his *World Authors*.
New York: H. W. Wilson, 1975, pp. 1076-1078.

Walston, Rosa Lee. "Flannery O'Connor: A Good Writer Is Hard to
Find." *Columns*, Fall, 1965, pp. 8-13.

Walters, Dorothy. *Flannery O'Connor*. New York: Twayne, 1973.

Warnke, Frank J. "A Vision Deep and Narrow." *New Republic*,
March 14, 1960, pp. 18-19.

Wedge, George F. "Two Bibliographies: Flannery O'Connor, J. F.
Powers." *Critique: Studies in Modern Fiction*, 2, No. 2
(Fall, 1958), 59-63.

Weisheipl, J[ames] A[thanasius]. "Thomism." *New Catholic Encyclopedia*. Vol. 14. 1967.

Wilder, Amos N. *Theology and Modern Literature*. Cambridge: Har-
vard Univ. Press, 1958.

Wray, Virginia. "Flannery O'Connor in the American Romance Tradition." *The Flannery O'Connor Bulletin*, 6 (1977), 83-98.

Wylie, John Cook. "The Unscented South." *Saturday Review*, June
4, 1955, p. 15.

INDEX